The Complex PTSD Workbook

Overcome Shame, Hypervigilance, Flashbacks, and Trauma Patterns Through Step-by-Step Healing Exercises

Rachel Singer

Table of Contents

About Me and Why I Wrote This Book

I was thirty-two years old, sitting in my car in a parking lot, when I realized I'd been holding my breath for most of my life.

Not literally. My lungs worked fine. But my chest was always tight, my shoulders always up near my ears, my jaw always clenched. I was driving home from a coffee meeting with a friend who'd said something completely innocuous: "You seem stressed lately." I'd spent the next twenty minutes in my car replaying the conversation, convinced I'd said something wrong, that they were upset with me, that I'd revealed too much or not enough or been too intense or not present enough. My hands were shaking on the steering wheel.

This was normal for me. This was every day.

I didn't know it was C-PTSD. I didn't even know what C-PTSD was.

I'd spent my twenties thinking I just needed to work harder on myself. I read every self-help book I could find. I tried meditation apps that told me to "just breathe" and "be present," which made me feel worse because I couldn't do either without my nervous system screaming. I went to therapy and talked about my anxiety, my perfectionism, why I couldn't maintain relationships. My therapist was kind, but we kept circling the same issues without ever landing on why my body felt like a live wire all the time.

I was functional. I had a job. I paid my bills. From the outside, I looked fine. But inside, I was running on fumes, managing a constant low-grade panic that occasionally spiked into full crisis for reasons I couldn't name. I couldn't relax. I couldn't trust people. I pushed away anyone who got too close and then felt devastated by the loneliness. I had an inner voice that told me I was fundamentally defective, and I believed it completely.

The worst part was that I couldn't point to a single traumatic event. There was no car accident, no assault, no clear before-and-after. My childhood was just difficult. Unpredictable. Emotionally cold in some ways, chaotic in others. I learned early that my feelings didn't matter, that asking for help was a burden, that I needed to stay small and manage everyone else's emotions if I wanted to be safe. But because there was no dramatic incident to point to, I thought I had no right to call it trauma. I thought I was just weak, too sensitive, not trying hard enough to get over it.

Then I found an article about Complex PTSD.

It was three in the morning. I'd been awake for hours, my brain running through every interaction I'd had that week, cataloging my failures, predicting disasters. I was scrolling through my phone, looking for anything to quiet my mind, and I found a description of emotional flashbacks. Sudden, overwhelming feelings of shame, terror, or helplessness with no clear trigger. No images, no memories, just the emotional state of a frightened child dropped into your adult body.

I sat up in bed. My hands were shaking again, but this time it was recognition, not panic.

This was what I'd been experiencing my entire adult life. The sudden waves of shame that made me want to disappear. The terror that came out of nowhere when someone's tone shifted slightly. The crushing certainty that I was about to be abandoned or rejected, even when nothing in reality supported that belief. I wasn't overreacting. I wasn't weak. I was having flashbacks.

I spent the rest of that night reading everything I could find about C-PTSD. The hypervigilance. The inner critic. The freeze response. The relationship patterns. The difficulty with boundaries. Every single symptom described something I'd been living with for as long as I could remember. For the first time in my life, I had a framework that actually explained what was happening in my body.

But here's what frustrated me: most of what I found was either too clinical or too vague. Academic papers full of terminology I had to Google. Self-help books that told me to practice self-compassion without explaining how to do that when your nervous system is in crisis. Therapy modalities that required resources I didn't have. I wanted something practical. Something I could use immediately when I was in the middle of a flashback at 2 a.m. or dissociating in a meeting or spiraling after a minor conflict with a friend.

I started experimenting. I read research on polyvagal theory, somatic experiencing, attachment theory. I tried different grounding techniques until I found ones that actually worked for my nervous system. I learned to recognize my flashback patterns, to interrupt my inner critic, to see the early signs of shutdown or overwhelm. It wasn't linear. I failed constantly. I still fail. But slowly, things started to shift.

During this time, I discovered there were countless people quietly navigating experiences just like mine. Online forums, support groups, late-night conversations with friends who'd been holding similar stories without names for them. We were all trying to make sense of our nervous systems, all looking for tools that didn't feel impossible to use when things were falling apart. Those exchanges mattered. They were a lifeline. They were the first real evidence that I wasn't alone, and that none of us were "broken" for struggling the way we did.

Again, I'm not a therapist. I'm not an academic researcher. I'm someone who survived a childhood that taught my nervous system to never fully relax, and then spent years learning how to teach it something different. I've done the work. I'm still doing the work. I probably always will be. But I've learned enough to know that healing is possible, even when you can't remember what you're healing from. Even when you don't have a clear traumatic event to process. Even when you feel like you've been broken for so long that this is just who you are.

I still have hard days. I still catch myself scanning for threats when I'm safe. I still have to talk back to my inner critic more often than I'd like. But I also sleep through the night most of the time now. I have relationships where I can be myself without constant fear of abandonment. I can recognize when I'm having a flashback and bring myself back to the present. My body doesn't feel like an enemy anymore.

It feels like something I can work with.

This book is everything I wish I'd had when I first learned what C-PTSD was. It's practical, not theoretical. It's based on what actually works when your nervous system is dysregulated, not what sounds good on paper. It's written for people who need help now, not people who can spend years decoding terminology or sifting through clinical language that doesn’t speak to their lived experience.

If you've spent years feeling like something is wrong with you, if you've tried everything and still can't figure out why you can't relax, if you look functional on the outside but feel like you're barely holding it together, if you recognize even a fraction of yourself in these pages: this book is for you.

You're not broken. You're not too much. You're not beyond help.

Your nervous system learned to protect you in the only way it knew how. Now it's time to teach it something new.

I'm here because I've been where you are. I'm still figuring it out, just a few steps ahead. But I can show you what helped me find my way out of survival mode and into something that feels more like living.

Let's do this work together.

Introduction

"Trauma is a fact of life. It does not, however, have to be a life sentence." — Peter Levine

You've probably spent years thinking something is fundamentally wrong with you. Maybe you can't maintain relationships the way other people seem to. Maybe you're exhausted from anxiety that never fully goes away, no matter how safe your life appears. Maybe you watch other people relax, trust without waiting for betrayal, and you wonder what's broken inside you that makes these ordinary things feel impossible.

You might feel like everyone else got a manual for how to be human and yours got lost in the mail. You look functional on the outside while inside everything feels chaotic, fragile, or too much. You've become an expert at hiding the storm because you learned early that showing it wasn't safe.

You might have tried therapy. You might have read books about anxiety, depression, or relationship problems. Some things helped temporarily. But nothing quite explained why you react the way you do. Why your body floods with panic when someone raises their voice. Why you freeze when you need to act, or explode when you meant to stay calm. Why you push people away right when they get close.

The problem isn't that you haven't tried hard enough. The problem is that most approaches assume your nervous system works the way it's supposed to. They assume you had a childhood that taught you safety, that your needs matter, that you're fundamentally okay.

If that wasn't your childhood, those approaches will only take you so far.

Complex PTSD develops differently than the PTSD most people know about. There's no single traumatic event to point to. Instead, there was an environment where the people who were supposed to protect you were the source of harm, or were absent when harm came. Where you learned that showing emotion got you punished, that asking for help made you a burden, that your only job was to stay small and manage the moods of the adults around you.

You might not remember much from your childhood. That doesn't mean nothing happened. It means your mind protected you in the only way it could.

Your nervous system adapted brilliantly. It learned to scan constantly for threats, to shut down emotions, to read faces with extraordinary precision, to become invisible or to please everyone. These adaptations kept you alive. Your body kept the score long before you had words for what was happening. It learned patterns you didn't consciously choose but had no choice but to adapt to.

They never turned off.

Now you're an adult. The immediate danger is gone. But your body doesn't know that. It still runs the same programs it developed in childhood. It still treats ordinary moments like emergencies, still believes that being visible means danger, that trusting means getting hurt, that relaxing means lowering your guard at the wrong moment.

This is what makes Complex PTSD exhausting. You're not just dealing with memories. You're dealing with a nervous system stuck in a war that ended years ago. It's confusing to have a life that looks stable on the outside while something inside of you feels constantly on the verge of collapse.

Many resources focus primarily on thoughts or single traumatic events. But your trauma lives in your body and in patterns built over years. You need tools that work with your nervous system, not against it. You need to understand why your body responds the way it does so you can stop blaming yourself for reactions to overwhelming circumstances. You need concrete exercises you can use immediately when you're in the middle of a flashback, when shame is crushing you, when hypervigilance won't let you sleep.

This workbook offers practical, body-based approaches built on evidence-based methods effective for Complex PTSD. You'll find tools to recognize and interrupt patterns before they consume your day. You'll learn regulation skills you should have developed in childhood but didn't. You'll discover how to work with shame, anger, freeze, dissociation, and relationship patterns that have kept you stuck.

The exercises are designed to be accessible whether you're in therapy or not, whether you have an hour or ten minutes. You can use them directly as you read. They treat your symptoms as protective adaptations that outlived their usefulness, not character defects that prove you're broken.

Healing from Complex PTSD isn't about returning to who you were before trauma. There is no "before" when trauma happened during your development. Healing is about becoming someone new. Someone who can feel emotions without being destroyed by them. Someone who can be in relationships without losing themselves. Someone who can rest without waiting for catastrophe.

Someone whose worth doesn't depend on being perfect, useful, or invisible.

You can't think your way out of trauma stored in your body. But you can teach your body that the danger has passed. You can update the threat-detection system running in the background of every moment. You can build a relationship with yourself that doesn't require constant criticism.

You don't have to rush this process. You don't have to earn it. You only have to begin.

Your body has waited a long time for someone to listen. You're here now. That's enough.

The work is here. Your body is ready to learn it can finally rest.

Chapter 1:
Your Nervous System Holds the Story Your Mind Cannot Tell

"The body keeps the score." — Bessel van der Kolk

You're sitting in your living room on a Sunday morning. Sunlight streams through the window. Your coffee is hot. No one is yelling. No doors are slamming. Nothing bad is happening.

Your heart is pounding anyway. Your chest feels tight. Your mind is scanning the room, the sounds from outside, the expression on your partner's face, searching for threats that don't exist. You can't name what you're afraid of, but the fear is there, thick and real and exhausting.

You've probably spent years trying to figure out what's wrong with you. Why can't you relax when you're safe? Why does your body react like you're in danger when you're just sitting in your own home? You've tried deep breathing, positive thinking, telling yourself to calm down. None of it touches this feeling.

Here's what you need to know: your nervous system isn't broken. It's doing exactly what it learned to do when you were young. During childhood, your brain figured out that staying alert, scanning for danger, and never fully relaxing kept you safer. Maybe it helped you read your parent's mood before they exploded. Maybe it helped you become invisible when you needed to be. Maybe it helped you survive emotional abandonment by learning to need nothing from anyone.

That alarm system saved you then. The problem is, it never learned to turn off.

This isn't about being too sensitive or weak. This isn't about lacking willpower or positive thinking. Your symptoms have a biological basis. Your body is telling a story your conscious mind might not even remember. Understanding how your nervous system works and what it's trying to protect you from is the first step toward changing your relationship with it.

Why You Feel Broken When You're Actually Protecting Yourself

Your brain has one primary job: keep you alive. Not happy, not comfortable, not thriving. Alive.

When you were growing up in an environment where the people supposed to protect you were also the source of threat, your brain adapted. If your caregiver's mood could shift from loving to rageful in minutes, your nervous system learned to track every micro-expression, every tone shift, every footstep. If showing emotion led to punishment or mockery, you learned to shut feelings down before they surfaced. If no one responded when you cried, you stopped expecting comfort and handled pain alone.

These weren't conscious choices. Your developing brain was solving a survival problem with the tools it had. The hypervigilance, the emotional numbing, the people-pleasing, the isolation—all of it made sense in that context.

You scan every room you enter because surprise used to mean danger. You struggle to trust people because the adults who were supposed to be safe weren't. You have trouble identifying your own feelings because tuning them out was how you survived. You push people away before they can leave you because abandonment was inevitable and at least this way you control the timing.

Every symptom you judge yourself for has roots in protection. Your nervous system is still doing its job. It just hasn't received the memo that the danger has passed.

You've probably spent years asking yourself the wrong questions. "Why can't I just get over it?" implies there's something wrong with your character. "Other people had it worse and they're fine" ignores the reality that trauma isn't a competition and nervous systems respond to what they experience, not to objective rankings of suffering. "I should be stronger than this" assumes strength means overriding your body's distress signals rather than learning to work with them.

The right question is: What is my nervous system trying to protect me from, and how can I help it recognize that I'm safe now?

Your hypervigilance isn't paranoia. Your emotional reactivity isn't drama. Your difficulty in relationships isn't a personality flaw. Your physical symptoms aren't imaginary. These are all evidence of a nervous system working overtime to keep you safe from threats that no longer exist.

The survival strategies that helped you make it through childhood are now interfering with your adult life. Your body hasn't figured out yet that it can stop fighting a war that ended years ago.

✏ EXERCISE: Mapping Your Protection Strategies

In the left column, write behaviors you judge yourself for. In the right column, identify how each might have protected you as a child.

Behaviors I Judge Myself For	How This Might Have Protected Me
Example: Avoiding all conflict	*Maybe it kept me from triggering anger*

Behaviors I Judge Myself For	How This Might Have Protected Me

The Difference Between PTSD and Complex PTSD That Changes Everything

If you've been in therapy before, you might have heard the term PTSD. Maybe you've even been diagnosed with it. But if the treatments designed for PTSD haven't worked, if exposure therapy made you worse instead of better, if processing your trauma memories didn't bring the relief everyone promised, there's a reason.

You might not have PTSD. You might have Complex PTSD.

PTSD typically develops after a single traumatic event or a series of discrete incidents. A car accident. A natural disaster. Combat. An assault. The trauma has a clear beginning and end. You can point to what happened. Treatment focuses on processing that specific memory, reducing its emotional charge, and helping your brain file it away as something that happened in the past.

Complex PTSD develops differently. It comes from chronic, repeated trauma that usually happened during childhood, when your brain was still forming its understanding of how the world works. The trauma was relational. The people who hurt you or neglected you were the same people you depended on for survival. There was no single event to process because the trauma was the environment you lived in.

A soldier with PTSD might have flashbacks to a specific firefight, complete with visual details and sensory memories. You might have emotional flashbacks where terror or shame crashes over you without any visual memory attached. You feel five years old again, but you don't know why. There's no scene to process because what damaged you wasn't a scene. It was years of emotional abandonment, unpredictability, or abuse.

The symptoms overlap, but Complex PTSD includes dimensions that standard PTSD doesn't capture. A pervasive sense that you're fundamentally damaged or worthless. Difficulty controlling your emotions, with intense reactions that seem disproportionate. Relationship patterns that repeat the same painful dynamics. Feeling disconnected from yourself, like you're watching your life from outside. Loss of meaning or direction, like you don't know who you are beneath the survival strategies.

Trauma during childhood doesn't just create painful memories. It shapes your sense of self, your ability to regulate emotions, and your template for relationships.

You might have been diagnosed with depression, anxiety, bipolar disorder, borderline personality disorder, or ADHD at different points. Those diagnoses capture pieces of what you experience, but they miss the underlying cause. If you've tried multiple treatments without lasting relief, the treatment wasn't designed for your specific type of trauma.

Standard PTSD protocols focus on memory processing. Complex PTSD requires rebuilding your sense of safety, learning emotional regulation from scratch, and addressing the relational wounds that single-event trauma doesn't create.

✎ EXERCISE: Recognizing Your C-PTSD Pattern

Check the symptoms you experience:

PTSD Symptoms:

☐ Flashbacks with clear visual or sensory details
☐ Nightmares that replay specific traumatic events
☐ Avoiding places/people that remind me of trauma
☐ Feeling on edge or easily startled
☐ Intrusive thoughts about specific events

C-PTSD Symptoms:

☐ Emotional flashbacks (intense feelings without clear memories)
☐ Deep shame or feeling fundamentally flawed
☐ Difficulty controlling emotional reactions
☐ Stuck or painful relationship patterns
☐ Feeling disconnected from myself or unreal
☐ Not knowing who I am or what I want

What does it feel like to see your experiences reflected here?

____

____

____

____

____

How Childhood Trauma Rewires Your Brain and Body

Your brain built itself around the environment you grew up in. That's what brains do. They adapt.

A child raised in a safe, predictable home develops a nervous system that generally trusts the world.

Their amygdala, the part of the brain that detects threats, activates when there's real danger and settles when the danger passes. Their prefrontal cortex, which handles reasoning and emotional regulation, develops the capacity to calm the amygdala down when it overreacts. Their hippocampus properly time-stamps memories so they know the difference between past and present.

Your brain built itself differently. Your amygdala became hypersensitive, detecting danger everywhere. Missing a real threat in your environment could mean emotional or physical harm. Better to have a thousand false alarms than to miss the one moment when your parent's mood shifted and you needed to disappear. That sensitivity persists in adulthood. Your threat detection system still operates as if danger lurks around every corner.

Your prefrontal cortex didn't receive the developmental support it needed. When a brain constantly focuses on survival, it prioritizes the amygdala over higher-order thinking. You might struggle with emotional regulation because that part of your brain didn't get the nurturing and safety required to develop fully.

Your hippocampus can have trouble distinguishing past from present. A tone of voice that resembles your father's makes your heart race. A certain kind of conflict feels like annihilation rather than disagreement. Your brain responds to an old threat as if it's happening now.

Your nervous system has three basic states. Think of them as gears.

The sympathetic nervous system is your gas pedal. It activates when you need to respond to danger. Fight or flight. Heart rate increases, muscles tense, digestion slows, all your resources go toward dealing with the threat. This is supposed to be temporary.

The parasympathetic nervous system is your brake. It kicks in when the danger passes. Heart rate slows, breathing deepens, digestion resumes, you can rest and connect with others. You're supposed to spend most of your time here.

The dorsal vagal system is your emergency brake. When a threat is inescapable, when fighting or fleeing won't work, this system shuts you down. Freeze. Dissociate. Go numb. It's a last-resort survival mechanism.

In Complex PTSD, these systems don't function properly. Your gas pedal gets stuck on. You live in chronic activation, always scanning, always tense. Or your emergency brake engages too often. You go numb, disconnect from your feelings, watch your life happen from a distance.

Sometimes you swing between these states. Anxiety and hypervigilance one day, total shutdown the next. Your body tries to manage an overactive threat response without the tools to find balance.

Your physical body pays the price. Chronic pain, digestive issues, autoimmune conditions, insomnia, fatigue—all connected to a nervous system stuck in survival mode. When your body thinks threat is constant, it redirects resources away from healing and maintenance. Inflammation increases. Stress hormones stay elevated. Your immune system can turn on itself.

Your brain is plastic. Neuroplasticity means the patterns that formed can change. The neural pathways keeping you stuck can be rewired through consistent, targeted healing practices. Your brain spent years adapting to danger. It will take time to adapt to safety. But it can happen.

EXERCISE: Your Nervous System States Tracker

Hyperarousal (Fight/Flight): Racing heart, muscle tension, racing thoughts, on edge, irritable, can't sleep

Window of Tolerance (Optimal): Clear thinking, emotions manageable, connected to yourself/others, can respond vs. react

Hypoarousal (Freeze/Shutdown): Numb, exhausted, disconnected, brain fog, hard to move, watching life from outside

Circle the state you spend most time in: **Hyperarousal / Window of Tolerance / Hypoarousal**

What situations or triggers consistently push you into that state?

____

____

____

____

Reading Your Body's Signals Without Judgment

Your body has been trying to talk to you for years. You've probably been ignoring it.

During trauma, listening to your body didn't help. Fear didn't stop the abuse. Pain didn't make anyone protect you. Hunger, exhaustion, discomfort—expressing these needs often led to more harm. You learned to disconnect. You pushed through. You told yourself you were fine when you weren't. That disconnection kept you functional when you had no other options.

Now, as an adult, you might not notice hunger until you're shaking. You might not register exhaustion until you collapse. You might not recognize emotional distress until you're in crisis. The ability to sense what's happening inside your body, called interoception, has been compromised.

That tightness in your chest when you're anxious. The knot in your stomach before a difficult conversation. The tension in your shoulders when you're overwhelmed. These sensations are your nervous system's way of communicating. Your body is telling you something about your internal state, about how safe or threatened you feel, about what you need.

You've learned to treat these signals as problems to fix or ignore. The goal here is different. These sensations are data. They're information about what's happening in your nervous system. You don't have to make them go away immediately. You just need to notice them, name them, and let them tell you what they know. This probably sounds risky. Maybe you're thinking, "If I pay attention to what I'm feeling, I'll be overwhelmed." Maybe you don't trust your body. Maybe tuning into physical sensations makes you more anxious, not less.

Those concerns make sense. Your body has been holding unprocessed trauma. Opening that door all at once would be overwhelming. You're going to practice small moments of noticing. You're going to build your capacity gradually. You don't have to feel everything all at once. Start with sensations that feel neutral or mildly pleasant. The feeling of your feet on the ground. The temperature of your hands. The texture of fabric against your skin. These sensations won't trigger you. They're a safe way to practice paying attention to your body without activating your trauma response.

From there, you can start noticing sensations connected to emotions, but only when you feel resourced enough. That means practicing when you're relatively calm, not in the middle of a flashback or panic attack. You're building the skill in low-stakes moments so it's available when you need it. Learning to listen to your body rather than override it is part of healing. Reconnecting with it helps you feel like you inhabit your own life instead of watching it from outside.

EXERCISE: Body Sensation Check-In

Bring your attention to each area. Notice the sensation without trying to change it.

Jaw

What sensation do you notice? (tension, warmth, tingling, numbness, nothing)

____

Intensity (1-10): _____

If this sensation could speak, what might it say?

____

Shoulders

What sensation do you notice?

____

Intensity (1-10): _____

If this sensation could speak, what might it say?

____

Chest

What sensation do you notice?

____

Intensity (1-10): _____

If this sensation could speak, what might it say?

____

Stomach

What sensation do you notice?

____

Intensity (1-10): _____

If this sensation could speak, what might it say?

____

Hands

What sensation do you notice?

____

Intensity (1-10): _____

If this sensation could speak, what might it say?

____

Chapter 2: Emotional Flashbacks Are Not Weakness

"Emotional flashbacks are sudden regressions to the overwhelming feeling-states of being an abused child." – Pete Walker

The question comes through your phone screen. A friend asking if you're free next weekend. Your finger hovers over the keyboard, but something has already shifted inside you. The air feels thinner. Your ribcage contracts in a way you can't control, and suddenly you're convinced this person is about to tell you they don't want to see you anymore. The invitation isn't an invitation at all; it's the setup for rejection.

You type "Sure!" and hit send before the feeling can stop you, but your hands are shaking now. The certainty sits in your chest like a stone: they asked out of obligation, they'll cancel, they never wanted to be friends in the first place. You've become an inconvenience waiting to be discarded.

Nothing in the actual message suggested any of this. Yet here you are, drowning in abandonment so visceral you can taste it. You know, intellectually, that your response doesn't match the situation. That knowledge changes nothing. The feeling is bigger than logic.

This is what makes emotional flashbacks so disorienting. There's no scene playing in your mind, no visual memory of a specific moment from your past. You're not watching your childhood self get left behind at a playground or hearing a parent's voice saying you're too much trouble. You're just feeling it, all of it, with an intensity that seems to prove the feeling must be true.

When you were small and your caregiver was unpredictable about showing up, your nervous system recorded that experience not as a story but as a state: the terror of being left, the certainty that you don't matter enough to stay for. Your brain didn't have the capacity yet to create a narrative around it, to think "I'm scared because my parent is unreliable." It could only register "I am alone. I am in danger. This is what I am."

Those states live in your body now. When something in your present life brushes against them, even something as simple as a friend's text, they surface with the same force they had when you were too young to understand them. The adult you can see what's happening and still be unable to stop it. Your prefrontal cortex, the part of your brain that could remind you this is just a text message and your friend has never given you reason to doubt their intentions, simply can't compete with the amygdala's alarm.

People often spend years experiencing these overwhelming emotional states without understanding what they are. They think they're overreacting, being dramatic, revealing some fundamental defect in their personality. They build their lives around avoiding situations that might trigger these feelings, never realizing they're dealing with a specific, nameable trauma response that can be managed.

These flashbacks don't make you weak. They're evidence of how hard your nervous system worked to keep you alive when the people who were supposed to protect you didn't. The intensity you feel now is proportional to the danger you faced then, when you were small and dependent and had nowhere else to go.

Learning to recognize emotional flashbacks changes what they can do to you. You can't make them disappear immediately, but you can learn to catch them earlier, interrupt their trajectory, and recover faster. The feelings don't have to define your reality anymore.

When Past Terror Shows Up as Present-Day Panic

Your nervous system doesn't distinguish between remembering and experiencing. When something in your present activates neural pathways connected to childhood trauma, those pathways fire as if the original event is happening now. Your body floods with the same stress hormones. Your heart rate spikes or your breathing shallows. You feel what your younger self felt, but without any mental image to explain why.

The hippocampus, the brain structure that normally timestamps memories and marks them as "past," wasn't fully developed when many of these traumatic experiences occurred. If you were younger than three, or if you were under extreme ongoing stress that compromised your hippocampus's function, those experiences got stored differently. They became implicit memories: patterns and responses your body knows without your conscious mind having access to the original event.

This is why you can be standing in your kitchen making dinner when a cabinet door sticks, and suddenly you're hit with frustration so overwhelming it feels like rage. There's no logical connection between a sticky door and the magnitude of what you're feeling. But your body remembers being small and powerless, when nothing worked the way it should and you had no control over your environment. The stuck door isn't just a stuck door. It's every moment you were trapped and helpless, compressed into this single instant.

Traditional PTSD flashbacks have a sensory quality. The combat veteran sees the battlefield again, smells smoke, hears explosions. There's usually a clear "I'm back there" experience. The person knows they're remembering something specific, which, while terrifying, at least provides context.

You get no such clarity. The emotions arrive without identification tags. You feel worthless, so you believe you are worthless right now. You feel terrified, so you believe danger is imminent right now. You feel enraged, so you believe someone is attacking you right now. The feeling and the thought are fused. This is why emotional flashbacks are often more destabilizing than their traditional counterparts. At least with a sensory flashback, there's a boundary between then and now. With emotional flashbacks, the past becomes the present without announcing itself.

What triggers these responses can be obvious or nearly invisible. A raised voice might trigger you if your parent's anger preceded violence. That connection is traceable. But other triggers operate below conscious awareness. A particular quality of afternoon light that coincides with the time your parent used to come home. The rhythm of someone's footsteps in the hallway. A specific type of silence that feels too much like the quiet before an explosion. Your nervous system tracked these patterns when you were young, filing them under "warning signs," and it still responds to them decades later.

Sometimes the trigger is internal. You feel a flash of genuine need, wanting comfort or support from someone, and that vulnerability itself activates the alarm. Needing things in childhood was dangerous because it might have been met with anger, mockery, or abandonment. Your adult need trips the same wire, and suddenly you're flooded with the certainty that asking for anything will get you hurt.

The body holds these memories in specific ways. Your jaw might clench without you realizing it, the same clenching that happened when you had to stay quiet to stay safe. Your shoulders might rise and tighten, preparing for a blow that isn't coming. Your breathing might become shallow and high in your chest, the breathing pattern of a child trying to be invisible. These physical responses happen automatically, outside your conscious control, because they're part of how the memory is stored.

What makes emotional flashbacks particularly cruel is how your inner critic uses them. You're already overwhelmed by feelings that seem to have no cause. Then that harsh internal voice arrives with its interpretation: "Why are you falling apart over nothing? Everyone else can handle normal life. You're fundamentally broken." The flashback becomes evidence for every terrible thing you believe about yourself. The critic doesn't recognize that you're having a trauma response. It thinks your reaction proves you're defective.

This creates a secondary wave of suffering. You're not just experiencing the original terror or shame from childhood. You're also experiencing shame about having the flashback in the first place. You feel weak for being so affected. You feel embarrassed that you're fighting tears in public over something you can't even name. You feel frustrated with yourself for "still not being over" your childhood. The original flashback triggers shame, which deepens the flashback, which triggers more shame. The spiral can consume hours or entire days.

Different people have different emotional signatures. Some people's flashbacks are dominated by fear: the visceral conviction that something terrible is about to happen, even when they're objectively safe. Others experience primarily shame: suddenly feeling exposed, disgusting, wrong in a way that makes them want to disappear. Some people get hit with rage that feels entirely disproportionate to whatever sparked it. This anger often confuses them because they're not typically angry people, but the fury is real. It's the anger they couldn't safely express as children, finally finding a crack to escape through.

Grief flashbacks are their own devastation. Something small happens, a minor loss or disappointment, and you're suddenly hollowed out by sorrow. You might find yourself crying and not entirely sure why. The tears are real. They're for the parent you needed but never had, the childhood that was stolen from you, the safety that should have been your birthright. The present loss is just the entry point. The grief is for everything you never got to mourn when it was actually happening.

Sometimes multiple emotions hit simultaneously. Fear and rage together. Shame and grief intertwined. The confusion of feeling everything at once adds its own layer of distress. You can't even name what you're feeling because it's too many things, all of them too big, all competing for space in your body.

You might not realize you've had a flashback until it's over. You snapped at someone, shut down in a conversation, or spent an evening numb and disconnected. Only later, reviewing what happened, do you recognize the pattern: the feelings were too large for the situation, your body went into survival mode, your thinking brain went offline. That retrospective recognition still counts. Each time you name a flashback after the fact, you're building the neural pathways that will eventually let you catch it earlier.

The goal isn't to never have flashbacks. The goal is to recognize them for what they are: old feelings surfacing, not accurate assessments of your current reality. That recognition creates just enough space between you and the overwhelming emotion to remember you have tools, you have options, you're not actually the helpless child you feel like in that moment.

Exercise: Naming Your Emotional Flashback Signature

Think of a recent time when intense emotions hit you fast. Use this space to track what happened in sequence, noticing the order things appeared.

What was the very first thing you noticed? (A thought? A body sensation? An image? A sound?)

____

____

____

What happened next? (Track the sequence: did the thought come first, then the body response? Or did your body react before you had words for it?)

____

____

At the peak, what emotion(s) were strongest?

____

____

What did you do in response? (Withdrew? Lashed out? Froze? Tried to push through it?)

Looking back now, does this sequence feel familiar? (Have you felt this same progression of sensations and emotions before?)

The point isn't to analyze why it happened. It's to start recognizing your specific pattern so you can catch it earlier next time. Your flashback has a signature, a particular way it moves through you. Learning that signature is your early warning system.

Recognizing Your Flashback Patterns and Triggers

Your triggers are as unique as your history. What overwhelms you might not affect someone else at all, and what devastates them might barely register for you. Your nervous system learned to scan for the specific dangers you actually faced.

Patterns emerge over time. A single flashback might seem random, but when you look at the last ten times you've been triggered, you start to see common threads. Not always the same external event, but the same underlying dynamic. The feeling of being dismissed. The experience of something not working the way it should. The moment when someone's attention shifts away from you. These patterns point back to what was most dangerous or painful in your childhood.

Sometimes a trigger is layered. Your partner sighs while you're talking, and you're suddenly certain they're annoyed with you, which makes you feel like a burden, which activates the belief that you're too much, which connects to every time you were made to feel your needs were excessive. The sigh wasn't the whole trigger. It was the entry point to a network of connected wounds.

Timing matters more than people realize. You might handle criticism fine on a Tuesday when you're rested and feeling secure. The same criticism on Friday after a stressful week when you're depleted might send you into a full flashback. The trigger hasn't changed. Your available resources have. When your nervous system is already taxed, your threshold for what you can handle drops dramatically.

Certain situations seem designed to activate old wounds. A pause in conversation that lasts two seconds too long, and you're convinced you've said something wrong. Someone cancels plans, and you're flooded with the certainty that they never wanted to spend time with you anyway. A partner seems distant for an evening, and you're positive the relationship is ending. The present situation might be completely innocent, but it rhymes with the past in a way your body recognizes before your mind catches up.

Your own internal states can trigger flashbacks. Feeling happy or hopeful might activate anxiety if good things in childhood were always followed by punishment or loss. Your nervous system learned that positive feelings are dangerous, that they set you up for disappointment. So when something genuinely good happens now, instead of feeling joy, you feel dread. Your body is trying to protect you from the inevitable crash it believes is coming.

Physical states change your vulnerability. Hunger, exhaustion, illness, or pain lower your capacity to regulate. You're more likely to flashback when your body is already stressed. This mirrors childhood, when you couldn't always meet your basic needs and had to depend on caregivers who were unreliable or hostile. Your depleted state now connects to your depleted state then.

Sometimes flashbacks cluster around specific times. Anniversaries of traumatic events can trigger you even if you're not consciously thinking about them. Your body remembers the season, the month, the quality of light at that time of year. Holidays that were tense or painful in childhood can trigger flashbacks even in safe adult contexts. Your nervous system is carrying information your conscious mind might not even have access to.

Tracking patterns doesn't mean avoiding everything that might trigger you. That's impossible and would require you to make your life smaller and smaller until you're living in a cage of your own making. The point of recognizing patterns is awareness. When you understand what tends to trigger you, you can recognize a flashback for what it is instead of believing the feelings are giving you accurate information about right now.

You can also start catching the early signs. Before a full flashback hits, there are usually subtle signals. A slight shift in your breathing. A feeling of distance, like you're suddenly behind glass. A hypervigilance that makes you track everyone's expressions and tone. These early signals are your opportunity to intervene before the flashback takes over completely.

Exercise: Your Flashback Trigger Map

Instead of analyzing each situation separately, look for the common thread connecting them. Think of three recent times you had strong emotional reactions.

Situation 1:

____

Situation 2:

____

Situation 3:

Now look across all three. What's the common element? (Not the surface situation, but the underlying dynamic. Were you feeling invisible? Controlled? Like you did something wrong? Like you were about to be abandoned?)

This dynamic in childhood looked like:

When I notice this dynamic starting now, my body's first response is:

You're building a map of your specific vulnerability. Not to blame your childhood or excuse your reactions, but to understand the logic of your nervous system so you can work with it instead of against it.

The 13-Step Protocol to Stop a Flashback in Its Tracks

You won't execute these steps perfectly. When you're in a flashback, your thinking brain is compromised. You might only remember one or two steps, or you might not remember any of them until hours later. That still counts as practice. Every time you work through these steps, even retrospectively, you're building neural pathways that make intervention possible.

Step 1: Say to yourself: "I am having a flashback."

Name it. Even if you're only 70% sure, say it. The act of naming brings your prefrontal cortex back online just enough to create distance. You shift from "I am worthless" to "I am a person having feelings of worthlessness." That distinction matters.

Step 2: Remind yourself: "I feel afraid, but I am not in danger. I am safe now, here in the present."

Your body is responding to a memory of danger, not current danger. You might need to say this multiple times. Look around the room and verify: there is no threat here. You are in your apartment, your office, your car. You are in 2025. You are an adult.

Step 3: Own your right to have boundaries.

Right now, you have options you didn't have as a child. You can leave this situation. You can say no. You can hang up the phone. You can ask for space. The powerlessness you're feeling is old. Your current reality includes agency.

Step 4: Speak reassuringly to your inner child.

This might feel awkward. Do it anyway. "I'm here with you. You're not alone anymore. I've got you. That was then; this is now. You don't have to be scared. I'm going to take care of us." Say these things out loud if you're alone, or silently if you're not. The child part of you that's terrified needs to hear from the adult part that can handle this.

Step 5: Deconstruct eternity thinking.

Flashbacks make everything feel permanent. "I'll always feel this way. Nothing will ever get better." Your brain has lost its sense of time. Counter that directly: "This is temporary. I've felt this before and it passed. This will pass too."

Step 6: Remind yourself that you are in an adult body with adult resources.

You are not the small child who couldn't speak up, couldn't leave, couldn't protect themselves. You can speak now. You can move. You can walk away. You can call someone. You have resources that were impossible then.

Step 7: Ease back into your body.

Use gentle grounding. Feel your feet on the floor. Notice what you're sitting or standing on. Press your hands together. Look around and name what you see: desk, window, tree, car, coffee cup. Touch something and notice its texture. The goal is to bring your awareness back to the present through your senses.

Step 8: Resist the inner critic.

Your inner critic will try to use the flashback as evidence. "See? You ARE broken. You CAN'T function normally." Talk back: "This is a trauma response. Having flashbacks doesn't make me defective. It makes me human."

Step 9: Allow yourself to grieve.

If tears come, let them. If you need to cry, cry. You're feeling what you couldn't safely feel as a child. Grief is how you metabolize loss.

Step 10: Cultivate safe relationships and seek support.

If you can, reach out. Send a text: "I'm having a hard time." Call someone who understands. Sometimes just hearing another person's voice helps your nervous system recognize you're not alone in danger. You're connected to safe people in the present.

Step 11: Learn to identify the types of triggers that lead to flashbacks.

This connects to the work you did in section 2.2. Keep tracking what situations tend to trigger you. Over time, this awareness lets you catch flashbacks earlier.

Step 12: Figure out what you feel.

Ask yourself: "What is this emotion?" Am I afraid? Ashamed? Angry? Sad? Lonely? Sometimes emotions are so tangled you can't tell them apart. The act of identifying and naming helps your brain start to regulate.

Step 13: Recognize the inner critic's voice and challenge it.

Notice what your inner critic is saying. "You're pathetic for falling apart." "Everyone else can handle this." "You'll never be normal." These aren't facts. They're learned scripts from childhood. You can start replacing them: "I'm not pathetic. I'm working with a nervous system shaped by trauma."

You don't need all thirteen steps every time. Some flashbacks need the full protocol. Others respond to just a few steps. Start with whichever steps resonate most. Maybe it's Step 1 and Step 2: naming the flashback and reminding yourself you're safe. Maybe it's Step 4, speaking to your inner child, combined with Step 7, grounding in your body. Make the protocol your own. Translate it into your language. Write it in a way that makes sense to you. The power isn't in perfect execution. The power is in having a structured response to what otherwise feels like chaos.

Exercise: Your Flashback Response Card

Create a reference card you can keep accessible: in your wallet, on your phone, taped inside a desk drawer.

Front of card:

I'M HAVING AN EMOTIONAL FLASHBACK

My 3 most helpful steps:

____

____

____

Back of card:

One grounding technique:

____

One thing I can say to the scared part of me:

One person I can reach out to:

You don't have to remember everything when your thinking brain is offline. You just have to remember to look at the card.

Building Your Flashback First-Aid Kit

The 13-step protocol gives you a cognitive framework, but when your prefrontal cortex is offline, thinking doesn't work. You need tools that bypass cognition and speak directly to your nervous system through your body and senses.

Your nervous system responds to input it can process: temperature, movement, texture, sound, smell. These aren't sophisticated interventions. They're simple, physical actions that interrupt the flashback response by giving your body different information.

The tools you need depend on your nervous system state during the flashback. Some flashbacks push you into hyperarousal: your heart races, you can't sit still, your thoughts spin. Other flashbacks drop you into hypoarousal: you feel numb, disconnected, frozen. Different states need different interventions.

For hyperarousal (when you're anxious, panicked, can't settle):

Cold interrupts a panic response fast. Splash cold water on your face. Hold ice cubes. Drink ice water slowly. The cold activates your vagal nerve, which signals your nervous system to shift out of emergency mode.

Intense physical sensation gives the activation somewhere to go. Squeeze ice cubes until they melt. Do push-ups against a wall. Stomp your feet hard on the floor. The physical intensity matches your internal state and helps discharge energy.

Rhythmic movement helps regulate. Rock back and forth. Walk at a steady pace. Dance to music with a strong beat. The rhythm tells your nervous system you're not frozen in threat.

For hypoarousal (when you're numb, shut down, disconnected):

Gentle movement helps when you feel frozen. Stretch slowly. Do simple yoga poses. Walk, even if it's just to the other room. You're reminding your body it can move.

Warmth helps when you feel cold and shut down. Hold a heating pad. Wrap yourself in a blanket. Drink hot tea. Warmth signals safety to a nervous system in conservation mode.

Bright light helps counter the shutting-down response. Open curtains. Go outside. Turn on all the lights. Light invites you back rather than shocking you back.

Texture gives you something to connect with. Hold something soft. Run your fingers over a smooth stone. Touch something with an interesting texture. Texture requires you to feel, which starts to bring sensation back online.

Universal techniques:

The 5-4-3-2-1 technique grounds you through your senses. Name five things you can see. Four things you can touch. Three things you can hear. Two things you can smell. One thing you can taste. This walks your awareness through all your senses, anchoring you in the present.

Bilateral stimulation helps regulate both activated and shut-down states. Butterfly hug: cross your arms over your chest and tap your shoulders alternately, left-right-left-right. Walk while noticing your feet alternating. The bilateral stimulation helps your brain process traumatic material.

Orienting is simple but effective. Slowly look around the room. Turn your head deliberately and notice what you see. This activates the part of your nervous system responsible for assessing safety.

Physical anchoring brings you into your body. Press your feet firmly into the floor. Push your hands together. Squeeze your arms or legs. The pressure gives your nervous system information about where your body is in space.

Environmental anchors:

Create a specific comfort object that becomes associated with safety. A particular blanket, a smooth stone you keep in your pocket, a photo. Over time, your nervous system learns to associate this object with being okay.

Designate a safe space in your home. A corner of a room, a specific chair, a spot outside. Somewhere you go specifically to regulate. Your nervous system learns that this space means safety.

What calms one person might agitate another. You need to experiment and find your particular tools. This isn't about finding the one perfect technique. It's about having multiple options.

The most common reason people don't use these tools is they forget they exist when they need them. This is why you practice when you're not in a flashback. Use your grounding techniques when you're calm. The more you use these tools in non-crisis moments, the more accessible they become when you're actually triggered.

Sometimes no single tool works. You try cold water; it helps a little but doesn't stop the flashback. So you add movement. Then you add a grounding phrase. Layering interventions is normal. Flashbacks are powerful. They might need multiple approaches.

You might feel self-conscious about some of these tools. Your nervous system doesn't care about sophisticated. It responds to what works. If holding a smooth stone at age thirty-five helps you come out of a flashback faster, that stone is medicine.

You won't always have access to all your tools. You can't splash cold water on your face in the middle of a meeting. This is why you need a range of tools, including ones that work in public: pressing your feet into the floor, using a breathing pattern, having a grounding object in your pocket, excusing yourself to the bathroom for two minutes.

The first-aid kit is about preparation. You're building resources before you need them. You're gathering tools so that when a flashback hits, you don't have to figure out what to do. You already know. You have a plan. You're not helpless.

✏ Exercise: Assembling Your Physical First-Aid Kit

Gather actual items and put them somewhere accessible.

Items to gather:

Something cold:

☐ Ice pack (store in freezer)

☐ Cold compress

☐ Other:

Something textured:

☐ Smooth stone

☐ Soft fabric

☐ Other:

Something scented:

☐ Essential oil

☐ Scented lotion

☐ Other:

Something grounding:

☐ Weighted item

☐ Stress ball

☐ Other:

Your flashback response card:

☐ Created and placed in kit

My designated safe space:

Location:

What makes it feel safe:

One person I can contact:

☐ I've told this person they're my support contact

One grounding technique I'll practice this week:

Technique:

When I'll practice:

Taking the time to physically assemble these items sends a message to your nervous system: I'm preparing to take care of myself. I'm building resources. I'm not powerless anymore.

Chapter 3:
The Inner Critic That Keeps You Small

"Perfectionism is the voice of the oppressor." — Anne Lamott

You're pathetic.

Everyone can see how damaged you are.

You'll never be normal.

Why do you even try?

You're wasting everyone's time.

You don't deserve good things.

You know this voice. It wakes up with you in the morning, narrates your day, and keeps you company at night. It's there when you look in the mirror, when you make a mistake, when someone compliments you. It tells you what you did wrong, what you'll never be able to do right, and why you should just stop trying.

This isn't an exaggeration. For many people living with C-PTSD, this brutal internal monologue is as constant as breathing. The cruelest part? You've learned to trust it. You've come to believe it's telling you the truth about who you are.

This voice acts like a terrified child trying to control what cannot be controlled. Children in traumatic environments develop an overdeveloped inner critic for a logical reason: if they can identify what's "wrong" with themselves, maybe they can fix it and finally earn love, safety, or approval. "If I'm bad, and I can become good, then the abuse will stop." This gives a child a sense of control in a situation where they have none.

Your critic kept insisting you were the problem because that story felt safer than admitting the adults failed you. Years later, decades later, it's still running the same program, attacking you for being human.

You can learn to recognize this voice for what it is. You can challenge it. And you can replace it with something that doesn't require you to be perfect to deserve kindness.

How Your Survival Mechanism Started Working Against You

Children believe everything is about them. A toddler thinks they made it rain by being sad. A five-year-old believes their parents divorced because they were naughty. This self-centered worldview is how young brains make sense of cause and effect.

When a child experiences abuse, neglect, or abandonment, their developing brain reaches a catastrophic but logical conclusion: "This is happening because something is wrong with me."

This self-blame serves several protective functions that help a child survive an impossible situation. It preserves attachment when a child can't afford to see their caregiver as dangerous. If the problem is the child who can theoretically change, rather than the parent who the child depends on for survival, hope remains possible. A child needs that caregiver to survive, so the blame turns inward to keep the bond intact.

Self-blame also creates a sense of control. "If I'm the problem, then fixing myself means things will get better" offers agency in a helpless situation. This feels less terrifying than accepting you're at the mercy of unpredictable or dangerous adults. By becoming hypervigilant about every potential flaw or mistake, the critic attempts to help you be "perfect enough" to avoid punishment, rejection, or abandonment. If you can spot your mistakes before anyone else does, if you can criticize yourself before they criticize you, maybe you can prevent the pain.

The messages your inner critic delivers today depend on what you survived then. Physical abuse taught you that you deserve pain, that you provoke people, that staying small and quiet might keep you safer. Emotional neglect created the belief that you're too needy, too much, that your needs drive people away. The critic attacks any sign of wanting something because expressing needs led to rejection. Sexual abuse instilled the message that your body is shameful, that you're fundamentally dirty. Abandonment produces the conviction that you're unlovable, that everyone leaves eventually, that you're not worth staying for. The critic preemptively rejects connection to avoid the pain of being left. Emotional abuse echoes explicit messages about your stupidity, your incompetence, your worthlessness.

In childhood, this voice might have actually helped you survive. It made you compliant when compliance kept you safer. It made you invisible when visibility was dangerous. It made you hypervigilant when missing cues could mean disaster.

But when childhood ends and the immediate danger passes, the critic doesn't retire. It intensifies. It has decades of practice now. It knows every vulnerability, every shame point, every fear. It sounds like truth because it's been the dominant narrative for so long. It feels like your own thoughts because it's been with you since before you had language to name it.

The critic attacks you for having needs. For making mistakes. For feeling emotions. For simply existing. It treats normal human experiences as proof of your fundamental brokenness. And because it sounds like you, because it uses your own voice, you believe it.

This part of you is still trying to keep a child safe from dangers that no longer exist. It doesn't know the war is over. It's still fighting battles from decades ago, using strategies that no longer serve you.

EXERCISE: Tracing Your Critic's Origin

Write down your answers to these questions. This is just for you.

What does your inner critic say most often? List 3-5 messages you hear regularly. Be specific. Write the actual words.

Whose voice does it sound like? Does it echo a parent, caregiver, teacher, sibling, or bully? Sometimes it's one person. Sometimes it's a mix. Sometimes it sounds like "you," but with someone else's words.

What might this voice have been trying to protect you from as a child? What bad thing was it trying to prevent? Punishment? Rejection? Abandonment? Harm?

What would have happened if you didn't have this critical voice monitoring you?

The Difference Between Healthy Self-Reflection and Toxic Shame

You need to be able to look at your behavior honestly. You need to learn from mistakes. You need to take responsibility when you've hurt someone or fallen short of your own values. Self-awareness isn't the problem.

The problem is that many trauma survivors have confused the inner critic's attacks with necessary self-awareness. They believe that brutal self-judgment is what accountability looks like. They think that if they stop attacking themselves, they'll become terrible people.

When you grew up being told that you were the problem, you learned to scrutinize yourself constantly. When love and safety were conditional on being "good enough," you learned to police every thought and action. The inner critic convinced you it was keeping you honest, keeping you humble, keeping you from becoming like the people who hurt you.

Picture this: you spoke harshly to a friend when they were trying to help you. Healthy self-reflection notices the specific behavior and asks what to do differently. "I snapped at them when they didn't deserve it. Next time I'm feeling defensive, I'll pause before responding. I can let them know I need a minute to process." You maintain your sense of worth while acknowledging the mistake. You look forward to what you can change.

The inner critic takes the same situation and attacks your core identity. "I'm a terrible person who ruins every relationship. I always destroy everything. There's no point in trying to change because this is just who I am." It erodes your sense of worth, dwells on the past without offering productive resolution, and provides no path to redemption.

Guilt says "I did something bad." Shame says "I am bad." Guilt focuses on behavior and can motivate positive change. Shame attacks identity and only creates suffering.

The inner critic uses shame as its primary weapon. It doesn't help you learn from mistakes. It convinces you that mistakes are proof of your defectiveness. It doesn't motivate improvement. It paralyzes you with the belief that improvement is impossible because the problem is who you are, not what you did.

The critic often disguises itself as helpful. When you think "I'm just being realistic," the critic is actually catastrophizing, turning one setback into evidence that nothing will ever work. That's prediction bias based on trauma, not realism. When you refuse to acknowledge your strengths because "I need to stay humble," you're not practicing humility. You're practicing self-erasure. Humility means remaining grounded while acknowledging what you do well. When you punish yourself endlessly with no possibility of redemption and call it "holding myself accountable," you're not practicing accountability. You're engaging in self-flagellation. Accountability involves acknowledging impact, making amends, and committing to change. When meeting 95% of your goals feels like failure and you call it "having high standards," you're not setting standards. You're setting traps. Standards are about what you're working toward. Perfectionism is about never being good enough.

The inner critic loves the word "should." You should be over this by now. You should be stronger. You should be able to handle this. Every "should" creates a gap between reality and an impossible ideal, a gap that generates constant shame. The word rarely reflects what's actually possible or reasonable. It reflects an imagined version of you that doesn't struggle, doesn't need help, and doesn't feel pain.

Healing doesn't mean you stop reflecting on your behavior. It means you develop an internal voice that's firm but kind, honest but compassionate, growth-oriented but patient.

EXERCISE: Rewriting Shame Into Growth

Take a recent self-critical thought and work through this process. Complete 3-5 examples.

Example 1

Inner Critic Said:

____

____

Is this shame (attacking who I am) or growth (addressing what I did)?

____

Compassionate Reframe: (Honest but kind. Focused on behavior and learning, not identity and judgment.)

____

____

Example 2

Inner Critic Said:

____

____

Is this shame or growth?

____

Compassionate Reframe:

____

____

Example 3

Inner Critic Said:

____

____

Is this shame or growth?

____

Compassionate Reframe:

____

____

Example 4

Inner Critic Said:

____

____

Is this shame or growth?

____

Compassionate Reframe:

____

____

Example 5

Inner Critic Said:

____

____

Is this shame or growth?

____

Compassionate Reframe:

____

____

Talking Back to the Voice That Says You're Defective

Talking back to the inner critic will feel unnatural at first. This voice has gone unchallenged for decades. It might feel dangerous to question it. What if it's right? What if you need this voice to keep you in line? What if removing this harsh oversight turns you into someone terrible?

These fears stem from the same flawed premise the critic uses: that you're only acceptable when you're being controlled. The critic doesn't keep you good. It keeps you small. It doesn't prevent you from harming others. It prevents you from living fully.

The goal is to reduce the critic's volume, frequency, and believability. To turn it from a deafening megaphone into background static you can easily dismiss.

Externalize the Voice

Stop saying "I am worthless" and start recognizing "My inner critic is saying I'm worthless." This creates distance. Some people find it helpful to give the critic a name or image: The Judge, The Perfectionist, The Drill Sergeant, The Bully. When you can picture it as separate from you, it becomes easier to recognize when it's active and to differentiate it from your authentic thoughts.

Question Its Evidence

The critic presents opinions as facts. Challenge it the way you'd challenge anyone making extreme claims without evidence.

Is this actually true, or is this an old story? The critic loves to replay narratives from childhood as if they're current reality. Just because someone told you that you were worthless 20 years ago doesn't make it true now.

Where's the evidence for this claim? If the critic says "Everyone thinks you're pathetic," ask for proof. Who is "everyone"? What did they actually say? Or is the critic mind-reading based on your worst fears?

Would I say this to someone I love? If your best friend made the same mistake you just made, would you tell them they're garbage who should give up?

Is this helping me grow, or just making me feel small? The critic claims it's motivating you. What does it actually produce? Growth or paralysis? Learning or shame spirals?

Identify Its Patterns

The inner critic has a limited playbook. It says the same things repeatedly, just dressed up in different scenarios. Once you recognize the patterns, they lose power.

You might notice the comparison game, where your internal experience gets measured against everyone else's external presentation. You see your own doubt and fear from the inside while seeing everyone else's curated competence from the outside. Or the fortune teller, predicting the future based solely on the past, ignoring every bit of evidence that you're capable of growth and change. The magnifier takes one mistake and transforms it into evidence of total inadequacy, one setback into permanent failure. The eraser dismisses successes as luck or meaningless while holding up failures as proof of your true nature.

When you recognize these patterns in real-time, name them. "Oh, there's the comparison game again." "The critic is fortune-telling." This simple act of naming reduces the thought's power.

Respond with Firm Compassion

You don't have to be nice to the critic, but you do need to be compassionate with yourself. You can be direct, even blunt, in refusing to engage with self-attack.

"Thank you for trying to protect me, but I don't need that kind of protection anymore."

"That's not true, and I'm not entertaining this conversation."

"I'm learning. Mistakes are part of growth."

"I deserve kindness, not cruelty."

Recruit Your Adult Self

The critic speaks from the wounded child's perspective. It's terrified, hypervigilant, and convinced that any mistake will lead to catastrophe. Counter it with your adult wisdom.

Your adult self knows things your child-self didn't. You survived. You have resources now: financial independence, the ability to leave dangerous situations, support systems, coping skills. You're not helpless. You're not trapped. You're learning and growing.

When the critic says "You'll be abandoned if you're not perfect," your adult self can respond with evidence: "I have people in my life who love me despite my flaws. I've made mistakes before and relationships survived. Perfection isn't the price of belonging."

Extremely positive affirmations often backfire when the critic is loud. If your critic says "You're worthless" and you try to tell yourself "I'm amazing and perfect," your brain will reject it as obviously false. The gap between the criticism and the affirmation is too wide. You'll feel like a liar, and the critic will use your discomfort as evidence that you were right to attack yourself in the first place.

Aim for balanced, evidence-based truths. "I'm struggling right now, and that's okay. I have worth even when things are hard." "I made a mistake, and I can learn from it. Making mistakes doesn't make me defective." These statements don't require you to believe you're flawless. They just require you to accept that you're human.

Talking back to the inner critic gets easier with practice. The first hundred times, it might feel forced or fake. You might not believe the compassionate responses you're giving yourself. You're building new neural pathways. You're teaching your brain that there's another way to respond to perceived failure or imperfection.

Over time, the compassionate voice gets stronger. The critic's volume decreases. You'll still hear it sometimes, maybe even often, but it won't dominate your internal landscape the way it once did.

EXERCISE: The Inner Critic Dialogue

Write out a conversation between your inner critic and your wiser, more compassionate self. Choose one of the critic's common attacks and work through these steps. Complete 2-3 dialogues.

Dialogue 1

Inner Critic says:

____

____

____

I recognize this as which pattern: (Comparison game? Fortune teller? Magnifier? Eraser? Something else?)

____

____

The evidence against this is: (List concrete examples that contradict the attack. Not what you wish were true—what actually is true.)

____

____

____

____

My compassionate response is: (What would you say to a friend? Or what does your adult self know that your frightened child-self doesn't?)

____

____

____

Dialogue 2

Inner Critic says:

___

___

___

I recognize this as which pattern:

___

___

The evidence against this is:

___

___

___

___

My compassionate response is:

___

___

___

Dialogue 3

Inner Critic says:

___

___

___

I recognize this as which pattern:

___

___

The evidence against this is:

____

____

____

____

My compassionate response is:

____

____

____

____

Replacing Criticism with Compassionate Accountability

You might be thinking: "If I stop criticizing myself, won't I become lazy? Selfish? Irresponsible?"

This fear makes sense if you grew up in an environment where love and safety depended on being good enough. If kindness was conditional, you learned that you needed constant monitoring and correction to stay acceptable.

The critic convinced you that without its brutal oversight, you'd fall apart or hurt others.

Research shows that harsh self-criticism is one of the least effective motivators for behavior change. When people feel ashamed, they don't become better. They become stuck. Shame leads to avoidance, self-sabotage, and giving up. People who treat themselves kindly when they struggle are more likely to keep working toward their goals, not less.

You can hold yourself to standards and acknowledge when you fall short without attacking yourself for being human.

The inner critic approach: "You failed because you're incompetent." This leads to shame, paralysis, and avoidance. The result? No growth. Just repeated patterns because you're too afraid to try again.

The compassionate accountability approach: "This didn't work. What can I learn? What will I do differently?" This leads to curiosity, problem-solving, and action. The result? Actual growth and change.

Self-compassion means acknowledging difficulty without dramatizing it. "This is hard right now" instead of "This is impossible and I can't handle it." It means treating yourself with the kindness you'd show a friend, using kinder language without lowering standards. It means recognizing that everyone struggles, everyone makes mistakes, that you're having a normal human experience. It means taking responsibility for your actions while maintaining self-worth. "I hurt someone and I need to make it right" instead of "I'm a monster who destroys everything." It means setting boundaries to protect your wellbeing, saying no when you need to, resting when you're exhausted, asking for help when you're overwhelmed.

Self-compassion doesn't mean making excuses or avoiding responsibility. It doesn't mean letting yourself harm others without consequence. It doesn't mean refusing to reflect on your behavior. It doesn't mean self-pity or victim mentality.

It doesn't mean permissiveness that enables self-destructive behavior.

Self-compassion creates a safe enough internal environment that you can push yourself, try new things, and risk failure because you know you won't destroy yourself if things don't work out. The critic makes you play it safe to avoid attacks. Compassion gives you the courage to grow.

Think of building an internal coach to replace the critic. A good coach sees your potential and believes in your ability to grow. A coach acknowledges when things are hard without pretending they should be easy. A coach offers encouragement.

A coach helps you learn from mistakes instead of proving you're defective. A coach celebrates progress, not just perfection. A coach knows that growth takes time and setbacks are normal.

When you mess up, your internal coach doesn't say "Great job!" It says "Okay, what happened here? What can we learn? How do we move forward?" It's honest about the mistake without making the mistake evidence of your worthlessness.

When you're struggling, your internal coach doesn't say "You're weak for finding this hard." It says "This is challenging. What support do you need? How can we break this down into smaller steps?"

When you succeed, your internal coach doesn't dismiss it. It acknowledges the accomplishment and the effort that went into it.

The shift from critic to coach takes time. You've been listening to one voice for decades. Building a new one requires consistent practice.

Every time you choose to respond to yourself with firmness and kindness instead of cruelty, you're strengthening that new voice.

Every time you acknowledge difficulty without attacking yourself for having difficulty, you're changing the relationship you have with yourself.

EXERCISE: Your Compassionate Coach Script

Write out how a compassionate coach would respond to situations where your inner critic typically attacks. Use these scenarios or create your own based on situations where you struggle most.

Scenario 1: You made a mistake at work

Critic would say:

____

____

____

Compassionate coach says:

____

____

____

____

Scenario 2: You snapped at someone you care about

Critic would say:

____

____

____

Compassionate coach says:

____

____

____

____

Scenario 3: You're struggling with something that seems easy for others

Critic would say:

Compassionate coach says:

Scenario 4: The critic used "should" on you (Example: "You should be over this by now" or "You should be able to handle this")

Critic would say:

Compassionate coach says:

Keep these scripts somewhere you can access them easily. When the critic starts up, you'll have specific, concrete responses ready. Over time, these responses will become more automatic.

Chapter 4: Shame Lives in the Body, Not Just the Mind

"Shame is the intensely painful feeling that we are unworthy of love and belonging." — Brené Brown

Your face burns. Your chest tightens. You want to disappear, to fold in on yourself until you take up no space at all. These sensations arrive before any coherent thought forms, hijacking your nervous system with a message that feels older than memory: you shouldn't exist.

This is shame. Not the brief discomfort of making a mistake, but the visceral conviction that your very being is wrong.

For someone healing from complex trauma, shame doesn't visit occasionally and leave. It sits in your body like a permanent resident, sometimes humming quietly in the background, sometimes screaming so loud you can't hear anything else.

Shame is a language your body learned early, before you had words for what was happening. It became the baseline hum of your nervous system, the default posture you collapse into, the reason you can't hold eye contact even when someone looks at you with kindness.

This chapter shows you where that body-based shame originated, how to recognize its physical signatures, and most important, how to release it through practices that work with your nervous system directly. You'll learn to approach shame not as something to think away, but as something to feel through and gradually discharge from your tissues.

What you learned can be unlearned, but that work requires addressing both the beliefs in your mind and the sensations locked in your body.

Understanding Why You Feel Fundamentally Wrong

Physical abuse teaches: "I'm bad. I deserve pain. Something about me provokes violence."

Sexual abuse teaches: "I'm dirty. My body is shameful. I caused this somehow."

Emotional neglect teaches: "I'm too much. I need too much. I should require less, or disappear entirely."

Emotional abuse teaches: "I'm stupid. I can't do anything right. I'm a burden."

Abandonment teaches: "I'm unlovable. Something about me makes people leave."

These aren't conscious thoughts. They're implicit beliefs that encode in the nervous system before language fully develops, becoming the foundation of identity.

Every type of childhood trauma comes with its own shame message, a specific variation on the same core theme: something is fundamentally wrong with you. The exact flavor depends on what happened, but the underlying conviction remains constant—you are defective at your core.

Children have egocentric brains. When a parent hurts them, ignores them, or can't meet their basic needs, children don't think, "This adult has their own trauma or limitations." Their brains make a simpler calculation: "If my parent can't love me, I must not be worth loving."

This conclusion gets encoded as body-based knowing. Your shoulders learned to round forward. Your voice learned to get small. Your eyes learned to look down. Your stomach learned to clench. These physical patterns became your default way of existing in the world, signaling to yourself and others: I am ashamed.

Shame feels like truth because it formed before you had a prefrontal cortex that could evaluate beliefs critically. It got wired into your brain as fact during a period when your brain was literally being shaped by your environment. It feels true the same way your native language feels "right"—it was learned at a foundational level.

Most people experience behavioral shame occasionally: "I did something wrong and I feel bad about it." This passes once you make amends or learn from the mistake.

People with complex trauma experience identity-level shame: "I am wrong. My existence is the problem." This type of shame doesn't respond to evidence or reassurance because it's not based on what you did. It's based on what you believe you are.

When someone tells you that you're worthy, kind, or talented, and you can't absorb their words—that's identity-level shame blocking the information. Your nervous system runs a program that says, "That might be true for other people, but not for me." The program is so old and so deep that contradicting evidence bounces off it.

These shame messages didn't form in a single moment. They accumulated through thousands of small interactions, glances, tones of voice, silences, absences. Your body absorbed them before your mind could make sense of them, storing them as muscle memory, as the way you hold your face, as the automatic impulse to make yourself smaller when someone's attention lands on you.

✏ EXERCISE: Your Shame Story

This exercise helps you identify your core shame belief and begin to see it as learned, not true.

What is your core shame belief about yourself?

Complete this sentence: *I am* _________________

(Examples: unlovable, defective, too much, disgusting, worthless, broken, wrong)

When did you first learn this about yourself? What age were you? What was happening?

Where do you feel this belief in your body right now? (Face, throat, chest, stomach, shoulders, overall sense of wanting to hide)

What happens to your body when this belief gets activated? (Posture changes, breathing, facial expression, eye contact)

The Childhood Logic That Turned Abuse Into Self-Blame

Every abused child faces an impossible cognitive problem. They hold two pieces of information that can't both be true:

"I am a good child who deserves love and protection."

"The people who are supposed to love and protect me are hurting me, ignoring me, or rejecting me."

A child's survival depends on their caregivers. The attachment system won't allow them to believe their caregivers are dangerous or unavailable. So they resolve the contradiction by rejecting the first belief: "I must not be a good child who deserves love. There must be something wrong with me."

Therapist Jim Knipe calls this the "bad child fantasy." The child creates a story where they deserve the abuse because this story offers hope: if they're bad, maybe they can become good, and then the abuse will stop.

You may have spent your entire childhood trying to become good enough—perfect grades, never making mistakes, anticipating everyone's needs, taking up less space, achieving more. None of these strategies worked because the problem was never you.

Shame doesn't just live in your thoughts. It gets passed down through bodies. A parent who was raised with shame carries it in their posture, their tone, the way they avert their gaze or stiffen when touched.

They transmit it through micro-expressions before a word is spoken—a wince when you speak, a barely perceptible pulling away, a look that says you're too much.

Children read these body signals with exquisite precision. You learned shame not primarily through what was said to you, but through how your presence was received physically. The way your mother's face tightened when you entered the room. The way your father's body went rigid when you asked for attention. The way you were looked at—or more accurately, not looked at.

These patterns became your patterns. You learned to tighten your face, to make your body rigid, to look away from yourself.

To start loosening shame's grip, you'll need more than insight. You'll need to work with the body directly, where shame actually lives.

EXERCISE: The Child's Impossible Choice

This exercise creates compassionate distance between your adult self and the child who first learned shame.

Part 1: The Child's Dilemma

Picture yourself as a child, at the age when you first learned you were "wrong."

What would it have meant for that child to accept that your caregiver was dangerous, unavailable, or incapable of love?

____

____

____

Part 2: From Your Adult Perspective

Complete this sentence:

The child I was chose to believe ____

about themselves because accepting the truth—that ____________________________________

____ *would have been unbearable.*

Part 3: Your Body Now

When you picture that child making this impossible choice, what does your body do right now?

(Notice: posture, breathing, face, eyes, throat, chest)

Releasing Shame Through Somatic Awareness

Shame lives in the collapse of your posture. In the heat spreading across your face. In the constriction of your throat that makes speaking nearly impossible. In the way your shoulders round forward as if to shield something vulnerable. In the impulse to make yourself smaller, to take up less space, to become invisible.

These aren't side effects of shame. They are shame.

You can understand intellectually that shame is a learned response. You can know that the abuse wasn't your fault. You can repeat affirmations about your worth. But if the shame is still locked in your tissues—in the way you hold your body, in your nervous system's default settings—it will continue to run its program regardless of what you tell yourself.

Working with shame requires approaching it gradually. You don't dive into your most intense shame all at once. That overwhelms your system. Instead, you start with manageable doses, building your capacity to feel and release shame without being flooded.

Locating Shame's Physical Signatures

Start by recognizing where shame shows up in your body. Bring to mind a mild shame experience—not your most intense one. Just something that triggers the feeling slightly.

Where does it appear? Your face might get hot. Your throat might tighten, making it hard to speak. Your chest might cave inward or feel heavy. Your stomach might twist or drop. Your shoulders might pull forward. You might feel an overall urge to curl up, hide, or disappear.

These locations are specific to you. Shame doesn't feel the same for everyone, but it does have consistent patterns within your own body. Learning your patterns is the first step.

The Practice of Staying With Sensation

Once you've located shame in your body, practice describing the sensation without judgment. Not "This feels terrible and I hate it," but neutral observation: "There's tightness in my chest." "There's heat in my face." "My shoulders are pulling forward."

This descriptive approach engages your thinking brain just enough to prevent overwhelm while keeping attention on the body.

Now breathe into that sensation. Not to make it go away, but to create space around it. Direct gentle breath toward where you feel the shame. Stay with it for 30 to 60 seconds.

Notice what happens. Sensations often shift, move, intensify, or dissipate when you give them attention without resistance. Track the changes without forcing anything.

Place a hand on the area where shame lives—your chest, your stomach—and speak to it: "I see you. I'm here with you. What you're feeling makes sense given what happened."

Countering Shame's Physical Collapse

Shame creates specific body patterns. You can work directly with these patterns to signal to your nervous system that you're not in danger.

Shame makes you collapse inward. Consciously uncollapse. Roll your shoulders back, lift your chest, raise your chin. This isn't about "fake confidence." It's about giving your nervous system different information: you're allowed to take up space.

Shame makes you avoid eye contact. Practice brief moments of gentle eye contact—with yourself in a mirror, or with a safe person. Even five seconds counts. This challenges the belief that you're too shameful to be seen.

Shame silences your voice. Practice speaking your truth out loud, even if just to yourself. Say: "I don't deserve shame. The abuse wasn't my fault. I have worth." Hearing your own voice say these words activates different neural pathways than thinking them silently.

Shame creates contraction. Any movement that opens and expands your body helps release shame from your tissues. Stretch your arms wide. Arch your back. Take up more space than feels comfortable. Stand up and plant your feet firmly.

These aren't affirmations or cognitive reframes. They're direct communication with your nervous system in the language it understands: body position, breath, muscle tension, spatial orientation.

EXERCISE: Somatic Shame Release

Use this practice when you notice shame activating in your body. Start with mild shame experiences and work up gradually.

1. Identify & Locate

What triggered the shame? (Keep it mild for this practice)

____

Where do you feel it in your body?

____

2. Describe the Sensation

Without judgment, describe what you notice (tight, heavy, hot, constricted, pulling, pressing, etc.):

____

____

3. Breathe & Stay

Take 3 slow breaths while keeping attention on that location.

Count them here: 1 _____ 2 _____ 3 _____

4. Compassion

Place one hand on the area where shame lives. Say out loud or silently:

"I'm here with you. This makes sense. You're safe now."

5. Counteract the Collapse

Do one physical action that opposes shame's pattern:

☐ Roll shoulders back and lift chest

☐ Raise your chin and make eye contact (mirror or person)

☐ Stretch your arms wide and take up space

☐ Stand firmly and plant your feet

6. Notice the Shift

What changed in your body after step 5?

____

____

____

Practice this with mild shame triggers once daily. Your nervous system is learning that shame doesn't have to be avoided—it can be felt, acknowledged, and released.

Building a New Identity Beyond the Trauma Story

For many people healing from complex trauma, shame isn't just a feeling they have. It's who they believe they are.

Your entire identity was built on the foundation of "I am defective, unworthy, wrong." Every decision you've made, every relationship you've entered, every career path you've chosen or avoided—all of it filtered through this core belief about yourself.

Healing requires building a sense of self that includes the trauma but isn't defined by it.

You are a person who experienced terrible things that weren't your fault. You are also more than what happened to you. The trauma happened and you survived. You were hurt and you have strengths. You carry wounds and you have capacity for growth. You've struggled and you've shown resilience. You have pain and you have worth.

These truths coexist.

"But this feels fake. The shame story feels real."

It feels real because your body has been living it longer. Your nervous system has practiced the shame response thousands of times. But longevity doesn't equal accuracy. The shame story is an old interpretation—one that made sense when you were a powerless child but doesn't reflect reality now.

Identifying Yourself Beyond Wrongness

Shame tells you that "wrong" is the core of your identity. Building a new identity means discovering what else is true.

You wouldn't have survived this far without strength. What got you through? Resourcefulness, determination, adaptability, intelligence, humor, the ability to read situations quickly. These aren't incidental traits. They're part of who you are.

When you're not in survival mode, what matters to you? Connection, creativity, growth, justice, compassion, learning. These values exist in you independent of trauma.

You have preferences, talents, quirks, interests. What do you enjoy? What are you curious about? What makes you laugh? These aspects of self often get buried under shame, but they're still there.

You're more than a survivor. You might be a friend, a creator, a learner, a helper, a parent, a partner, an artist, a thinker, a worker. Trauma is part of your experience, not the totality of who you are.

Practice "I am" statements that don't center shame or trauma: "I am someone who loves dogs." "I am someone who's learning to cook." "I am someone who cares about fairness." "I am someone who's figuring out healing." These statements don't erase your history. They expand beyond it. You may even notice qualities that grew through surviving what you did—deeper empathy, clearer sense of what matters, increased ability to navigate difficulty. This doesn't mean the trauma was "worth it." It means you metabolized terrible experiences into something that serves you now.

"If I'm not the broken person, who am I?"

This fear is normal. Shame-based identity, while painful, is familiar. You won't lose yourself by letting it go. You'll discover who you've been underneath it all along.

EXERCISE: Your Expanded Identity Map

Fill in at least 2-3 items for each category.

Strengths I've developed (including through surviving trauma):

Values that matter to me:

Interests or curiosities I have:

Roles I hold (friend, parent, worker, learner, etc.):

Qualities I have that have nothing to do with trauma:

Things I'm working toward or curious about:

Now write one paragraph beginning with "I am someone who..." (Include at least 3 aspects of yourself that go beyond shame.)

Which of these aspects are hardest to believe when shame is loud? Circle 2-3 items that directly contradict your core shame belief.

Notice your body as you read your paragraph back. Any tension? Softening? Resistance? Where?

Each time you return to this map, you're giving your nervous system a different picture of who you are. The image you hold of yourself isn't fixed—it shifts based on where you place your attention.

Chapter 5:
Your Hypervigilant Body Thinks Danger Never Ended

"Trauma is not what happens to you. Trauma is what happens inside you as a result of what happens to you." — Gabor Maté

You're at dinner with friends. They're recounting a story about something funny that happened at work, and you're responding at the right moments, nodding, even contributing a comment here and there. But underneath that social performance, a different process is running.

You're reading micro-expressions. The friend across from you just shifted in their seat—did that mean they're uncomfortable? Bored? About to leave? Someone at the next table laughed too loudly—are they laughing at you? The waiter approached from behind and you tensed before you even knew why. You're tracking the emotional temperature of everyone at your table, running continuous threat assessments based on tone shifts, pauses in conversation, changes in posture. You're not just scanning the physical environment. You're analyzing the social field, predicting who might be upset, where conflict might emerge, what you need to do to keep everything stable and safe.

Your friends are relaxed. You're working.

This is hypervigilance operating at the interpersonal level. Not just watching for physical threats, but running predictive models of social danger. Those aspects matter too, but in this chapter we're focusing on how hypervigilance plays out in your thoughts and relationships. Your brain learned that reading people's emotional states correctly could mean the difference between safety and harm. A parent's mood shift from calm to explosive happened in seconds, and the child who could detect the shift early had more time to brace, hide, or fix whatever might have triggered it.

Now your adult nervous system applies that same hyper-analytical process to every interaction. It builds threat models based on incomplete information. It treats ambiguity as danger. It interprets neutral social cues as potential rejection or criticism because in childhood, missing those cues meant getting hurt.

The hypervigilance discussed here isn't primarily about scanning for exits or startling at loud noises. This chapter focuses on the cognitive and social dimensions of hypervigilance—the constant mental surveillance that anticipates catastrophe, over-interprets social signals, and exhausts you with analysis of situations that don't actually threaten you.

Your hypervigilant mind is running outdated threat prediction software. It's trying to protect you by staying several steps ahead of danger that no longer exists. Learning to recognize when your brain is building false threat models and how to interrupt that process is what this chapter will teach you.

Why You Can't Relax Even When Everything Is Fine

Your thinking brain can assess a situation and conclude you're safe. You're at home. No one is angry. Nothing bad is happening right now. But your nervous system runs a parallel assessment that reaches a different conclusion: "Maybe not yet, but it's coming."

This anticipatory anxiety isn't irrational paranoia. It's a predictive system your brain developed to identify danger before it fully materialized. In childhood environments where threat was unpredictable, your survival advantage came from learning to read early warning signs. The child who noticed their parent's breathing change, or caught the subtle tension in their voice before anger erupted, gained precious seconds to prepare.

Your amygdala became specialized at pattern recognition for danger. It catalogued hundreds of micro-cues: facial expressions, vocal tones, body language shifts, environmental changes. It learned to ask not "Am I in danger right now?" but "What danger is about to happen?"

The problem is specificity. Your amygdala learned patterns in one context—your childhood environment with specific people—and now applies those patterns everywhere. A colleague's brief silence triggers the alarm because silence preceded explosions at home. Someone crossing their arms activates threat detection because that posture meant you were in trouble. Ambiguous social cues default to negative interpretations because in your experience, assuming the worst and being wrong was safer than assuming the best and being unprepared.

This is what researchers call predictive threat modeling. Your brain constantly generates predictions about what's going to happen next based on past patterns. For someone with C-PTSD, those predictions are weighted toward negative outcomes. In your nervous system's math, one missed threat counts more than fifty false alarms.

The physical cost shows up as chronic tension that doesn't match your environment. Your jaw stays clenched during pleasant conversations. Your shoulders remain elevated while you're sitting alone in your apartment. Your stomach churns when you're doing routine tasks. This constant low-level activation burns through energy even when you're "resting," which is why you can feel exhausted despite doing nothing particularly demanding.

The cognitive load is equally taxing. Part of your attention is always occupied with threat monitoring. You're analyzing conversations for hidden meanings, replaying interactions to check for errors, planning responses to problems that might never occur. This background processing makes concentration difficult. Tasks that require full attention become frustrating because you can't give full attention to anything while part of you is always on watch.

For many people with C-PTSD, letting go of vigilance feels dangerous in itself. The hypervigilance has become so woven into your identity that its absence triggers anxiety. "If I'm not anticipating problems, I won't see them coming. If I'm not analyzing social interactions, I'll miss important signs. If I'm not preparing for the worst, I'll be caught off guard." The vigilance feels like the only thing standing between you and catastrophe.

This is the bind: you can't rest because resting feels unsafe, but you can't function well because you never rest. The hypervigilance that was supposed to protect you has become the thing you need protection from.

EXERCISE: Mapping Your Hypervigilance Patterns

Part 1: Cognitive Hypervigilance

Check all that apply:

☐ Constantly predicting what could go wrong

☐ Replaying conversations to analyze for problems

☐ Planning responses to situations that haven't happened

☐ Difficulty enjoying present moments due to future worrying

☐ Creating worst-case scenarios automatically

☐ Second-guessing decisions repeatedly

Part 2: Social Hypervigilance

Check all that apply:

☐ Reading micro-expressions and tone for signs of displeasure

☐ Assuming people are upset with you without evidence

☐ Interpreting ambiguous social cues negatively

☐ Monitoring others' emotional states constantly

☐ Feeling responsible for managing others' emotions

☐ Exhaustion after social interactions from all the monitoring

Part 3: Reflection

What specific cues trigger your threat prediction system?

____

What disaster does your brain typically predict?

How often does the predicted disaster actually happen?

Your Social Tolerance Window

Beyond your internal emotional states, there's also a limit to how much contact with other people you can handle before your system starts to dysregulate. This is your social tolerance window. The window of tolerance applies not just to emotional activation but to interpersonal contact. Your capacity for social interaction gets compressed by hypervigilance, leaving you either overwhelmed by people or isolated from them.

Think of social tolerance as how much interpersonal contact you can handle before your system tips into overload or shutdown. For someone without significant trauma, this window is fairly wide. They can handle various types of social contact—intimate conversations, group settings, casual interactions, conflict—without leaving their regulated state. They can engage, disengage, and reengage fluidly.

For someone with C-PTSD, the social tolerance window is often very narrow. Even low-intensity interactions can push you toward dysregulation because your system treats social situations as high-stakes threat scenarios requiring intense monitoring and management.

Social Hyperarousal

When interpersonal contact pushes you above your window, you experience social hyperarousal. Your mind races through analyses of what people think, what they mean by what they said, what you should have said differently. You're hyperaware of every social misstep, real or imagined. You replay conversations, searching for evidence of how you failed or how others judged you. Your body stays activated hours after social interactions end, unable to downregulate because your threat detection system is still processing all the data it collected.

This state makes you hyperresponsive to social cues. A neutral facial expression reads as disapproval. Someone taking a moment to respond feels like rejection. Small talk feels dangerous because you're analyzing it for hidden meanings and judgments. You might talk compulsively, trying to fill space and control the interaction. Or you might perform friendliness while internally tracking every micro-signal of how you're being received.

Social Hypoarousal

When interpersonal load becomes too much, your system can flip into social shutdown. You withdraw, cancel plans, avoid messages. Being around people feels overwhelming not because of what they're doing but because of what maintaining the interaction requires from you. The constant monitoring, managing, analyzing—it's too much. Your system chooses disconnection as protection.

In this state, you feel numb in social situations. You're there physically but not present. You can't track conversations or feel connected to people. You might dissociate during interactions, watching yourself respond on autopilot. Or you avoid social contact entirely because the thought of engaging feels impossible.

The Social Window

When you're within your social tolerance window, interactions don't require hyperanalysis. You can be present without constant monitoring. Ambiguous cues don't automatically register as threats. You can tolerate normal relationship friction—disagreements, momentary disconnection, imperfect communication—without catastrophizing. You're able to trust that relationships can handle imperfection, including your own. The work of widening your social tolerance window involves learning to identify when interpersonal load is pushing you toward dysregulation and developing strategies to either stay within your window or return to it when you've been pushed out.

This is different from simply managing emotional states. This is specifically about the load that comes from being with other people and the hypervigilance that interpersonal contact activates.

EXERCISE: Tracking Your Social Window

Track for one week. Note daily:

Morning check-in:

State during social interactions: ☐ Hyperarousal ☐ Window ☐ Shutdown

Evening reflection:

What pushed me out of my window today?

____

How long did it take to feel regulated again?

____

End-of-Week:

What types of interactions keep me in my window?

____

What types push me into dysregulation?

____

Interrupting the Surveillance System

These tools target the specific mechanisms of hypervigilance—the predictive threat modeling, the social over-analysis, the constant environmental monitoring. They're designed to interrupt the surveillance system rather than just manage the aftermath.

Soft Focus Practice

Hypervigilance creates tunnel vision—intense focus on threat-relevant details while missing the broader context. This exercise widens your visual field to interrupt that narrow focus.

Sit comfortably and relax your eyes. Instead of focusing on any one thing, let your gaze soften so you're taking in your entire field of vision at once. Notice what's in your peripheral vision without turning your head. Let your eyes rest in this soft, wide focus for 2-3 minutes.

This works because threat scanning requires sharp, focused attention. Soft focus engages a different visual mode that makes detailed threat analysis harder to maintain. It signals your nervous system that intensive monitoring isn't required right now.

Naming the Non-Threat

Your attention gravitates toward potential threats. This exercise deliberately shifts attention to neutral and safe elements in your environment.

Look around and name five things that are definitely not threatening. "That plant is not a threat. This chair is not a threat. The book on the shelf is not a threat." State it out loud if possible. Repeat with different objects.

This interrupts the threat bias by training your attention on what's benign. Your amygdala learns through repetition that directing attention toward non-threatening stimuli doesn't result in harm.

The Prediction Check

When you notice yourself predicting a negative outcome, pause and make it explicit.

Write down:

"I'm predicting that ____ *will happen."*

Then: *"The evidence I'm using for this prediction is* ________________________________."

Then: *"The last time I made a similar prediction, what actually happened was* ____________________

____

This creates distance from automatic predictions by making them conscious and testable. Over time, you gather data about how often your threat predictions materialize, which helps calibrate your system toward accuracy rather than catastrophizing.

The What's Actually Happening Exercise

This exercise doesn't just ground you in the present; it specifically trains you to separate what is actually happening from what your surveillance system is predicting might happen. Hypervigilance operates in anticipated future threats. This exercise anchors you in present reality.

When you notice anxiety rising, ask yourself: "What is actually happening right now in this moment?" Describe only what's observable, not what you're predicting or interpreting. "I'm sitting at my desk. My computer is on. I can hear traffic outside. My hands are on the keyboard."

Reality-check your interpretation. Are you responding to something happening now, or to something your brain is predicting might happen?

Sound Distancing

Hypervigilance makes you reactive to sounds. This practice helps you evaluate sounds without immediately treating them as significant.

When you hear a sound, instead of reacting, pause and categorize it: Relevant or irrelevant? Close or distant? Requiring response or just background?

Most sounds are irrelevant background noise, but hypervigilance treats everything as potentially important. This exercise trains discrimination, allowing your system to filter out what doesn't need your attention.

Limited Analysis Windows

Hypervigilance analysis can continue indefinitely. This technique contains it.

When you catch yourself analyzing a social interaction or situation, set a timer for 5 minutes. Analyze as much as you want during that time. When the timer goes off, you're done. Move on.

This acknowledges the need to process while preventing the endless loop of reanalysis that exhausts you without producing useful insights.

EXERCISE: Building Your Interruption Toolkit

Choose 2-3 techniques from Section 5.3 to practice this week:

____

____

____

Daily practice time: ________

After one week:

Which technique worked best for interrupting your surveillance system?

Could you catch yourself earlier in the hypervigilance cycle?

Learning That Nothing Is Happening

The deepest work with hypervigilance isn't just managing activation when threats appear. It's teaching your nervous system to recognize when no threat exists at all—and that the absence of threat is real, not a temporary pause before danger returns.

This requires a fundamental shift. Your hypervigilant system operates on the assumption that safety is the exception and danger is the default state. It waits for the other shoe to drop. It treats peaceful moments as the calm before the storm. For healing to occur, you need experiences that challenge this assumption: moments where you deliberately notice that nothing bad is happening and nothing bad is about to happen.

The Absence Practice

Set a timer for 2 minutes. During that time, your only job is to notice what's not happening.

"Right now, no one is yelling at me. Right now, I'm not in physical danger. Right now, no crisis is occurring. Right now, I'm not being criticized or attacked. Right now, everything is actually okay."

This isn't forced positive thinking. You're not denying that bad things could happen later. You're simply acknowledging the reality that right now, in this specific moment, they're not happening. Your hypervigilance wants to argue: "But they could happen any second." That's true. And right now, they're not.

Practice this daily. Your nervous system learns through accumulation of experiences. Each time you pause to register the absence of threat, you're providing data that contradicts the always-danger assumption.

Tolerating Non-Vigilance

If hypervigilance has been your baseline for years or decades, deliberately letting it go—even briefly—can trigger anxiety. Your system interprets the absence of monitoring as danger itself.

Practice micro-moments of dropping vigilance in controlled ways. Choose a safe time and place. Set a timer for 30 seconds. During those 30 seconds, deliberately stop monitoring. Let your attention rest. Don't scan. Don't analyze. Don't prepare.

When the timer sounds, notice: Did the danger your system was anticipating materialize? You let your guard down for 30 seconds. What happened?

Gradually increase the duration. One minute. Two minutes. Five minutes. Your nervous system learns through experience that dropping vigilance doesn't lead to harm. The danger it was working so hard to prevent doesn't actually arrive when you stop watching for it.

The Safety Check-In Object

Choose one small object—a stone, a coin, anything you can carry easily. This becomes your "nothing is happening" anchor. This isn't a comfort object in the traditional sense. Its job isn't to soothe you, but to help you reality-check whether the danger you're preparing for is actually here.

Several times throughout the day, hold this object and ask: "What am I preparing for right now?" Let yourself name the threat your body is bracing against. Then ask: "Is that threat here right now?" If the answer is no, tell yourself: "Right now, nothing is happening. I'm preparing for something that isn't here."

The object becomes a cue to check reality against your predictions. Over time, touching it can trigger a quick recalibration: threat predicted or threat present?

Rewriting the Danger Script

Your hypervigilance runs on automatic scripts: "Something bad is about to happen. I have to stay ready. If I relax, I'll be caught off guard." These scripts feel like truth, but they're actually beliefs your nervous system formed based on past experience.

Write out the script your hypervigilance runs. Then write an alternative script based on present reality.

Old script: "I have to monitor everyone's mood or I'll miss danger signs."

New script: "I'm safe with people who don't require constant monitoring. I can choose relationships where relaxation is possible."

Old script: "Silence means someone is angry with me."

New script: "Silence is often just silence. I can check instead of assuming."

Read your new scripts daily. You're not trying to convince yourself to believe them immediately. You're introducing alternative interpretations so your brain has options beyond the default danger narrative.

Creating Controlled Low-Surveillance Zones

Designate specific times or places where you practice being less vigilant. Maybe it's the first 10 minutes after you wake up, or a specific chair in your home, or during a particular daily activity.

In that zone, you deliberately reduce monitoring. You don't scan for problems. You don't analyze interactions. You don't prepare for contingencies. You practice being present without defense.

Start with very short periods in very safe contexts. The goal isn't to eliminate vigilance everywhere—

it's to prove to your system that monitored time and non-monitored time can both be safe, and that you can choose which mode to be in rather than being locked in hypervigilance constantly. You're not forcing yourself to be undefended everywhere. You're just experimenting with very small pockets of time and space where it's safe enough to practice being less on guard.

EXERCISE: Your Nothing-Is-Happening Practice

My daily "Absence Practice" time: ______________________________

My safety check-in object: ______________________________

My hypervigilance script:

What my system automatically believes:

____

Alternative script based on present reality:

____

My low-surveillance zone:

Time/place: ______________________________

Starting duration: ______________________________

After two weeks:

How often did I practice noticing "nothing is happening"? ______________________________

When I checked reality against my predictions, how often was I wrong? ______________________________

What resistance came up when practicing reduced surveillance? ______________________________

Chapter 6:
Breaking Free From the Freeze Response

"Sometimes the bravest thing you can do is thaw." — Unknown

You know you should move, speak, act, but you can't. It's not that you won't—it's that your body simply will not cooperate. You're submerged underwater while the world moves above you, unable to reach the surface. Or maybe it's different: you go through the motions—work, responsibilities, daily tasks—but you're not really there. You're operating on autopilot while the real you is buried somewhere deep inside, numb and unreachable.

Freeze is perhaps the most misunderstood trauma response. People who haven't experienced it think it's a choice: "Just do something. Just move. Just speak up." But freeze isn't a choice—it's a nervous system state that overrides conscious will. It's what happens when fight and flight aren't options, when the only way to survive overwhelming threat is to shut down.

Two types of freeze exist in C-PTSD. The first is acute freeze: the sudden, complete immobilization in the face of perceived threat. You can't speak, move, or think. This is what happens during traumatic events when fighting or fleeing isn't possible. The second is functional freeze, sometimes called chronic freeze. This one is more subtle and far more common. You're moving through life, accomplishing tasks, maybe even appearing highly successful, but you're emotionally numb, disconnected from yourself, operating from a place of shutdown.

Life feels flat, you're just going through motions, and there's a pervasive sense of being stuck even while appearing functional.

Freeze is particularly devastating for three reasons. First, it's invisible. Unlike fight—which shows up as anger or confrontation—or flight—which looks like running away or avoidance—freeze happens internally. Others can't see it, so they don't understand it. Second, it creates confusion that spirals into helplessness. "What's wrong with me? Why does my body refuse to cooperate?" Third, it disconnects you from life. Whether acute or functional, freeze prevents engagement, joy, connection, and growth.

This chapter will help you understand freeze as a biological response, not a character flaw. You'll learn to recognize when you're in freeze, understand why it happens, and most importantly, learn how to gently thaw out and reconnect with life.

Freeze is your nervous system's emergency shutdown when other options aren't available. It kept you alive when you had no other way to cope. But now it's keeping you from living. Learning to thaw—gently, gradually, safely—is what this chapter is about.

When Your Body Shuts Down and You Can't Move Forward

Freeze is an ancient survival response observed across mammals. When a prey animal is caught by a predator and can't escape, it goes into tonic immobility—playing dead. This serves multiple functions: the predator might lose interest, pain receptors shut down, and if the animal survives, the freeze response can disengage and allow escape.

In humans, freeze activates when threat is overwhelming and fight or flight won't work, when you're overpowered and resistance is impossible, or when the threat is relational—from someone you depend on—creating an impossible bind.

The dorsal vagal complex of the parasympathetic nervous system takes over during freeze, causing drastically reduced heart rate and blood pressure, muscle rigidity or limpness, shallow breathing, dissociation, inability to speak or move, cognitive shutdown, and emotional numbing. Your body essentially powers down to survive.

For children in abusive or neglectful environments, freeze often became the primary survival response. They couldn't fight an adult. They couldn't flee because they depended on caregivers for survival. Fighting back or running away might lead to worse consequences. Freezing made them less "present" for the abuse—a mental escape when physical escape was impossible.

If freeze was your primary childhood response, your nervous system developed around this state. Your system learned to shut down faster than others, building what feels like a quicksand threshold where even mild stress triggers complete immobilization. Now, situations that evoke minimal pressure can activate freeze—your body's ingrained pattern is to power down rather than engage.

Acute freeze is the complete immobilization in the moment. You can't speak, move, or think. It's usually triggered by specific overwhelming situations and it's obvious to the person experiencing it—terrifying and confusing.

Functional freeze appears different. You move through tasks, maintain responsibilities, maybe even excel at work—but internally, you're running on the absolute minimum. Emotional numbness and flatness dominate. Dissociation becomes your baseline state. You can work, socialize, accomplish tasks, but feel like you're present but disconnected from the controls of your own body.

After repeated overwhelm, the nervous system can get stuck in a chronic low-grade freeze state. You're not completely shut down—you can still function—but you're not fully online either. It's like running in energy-saving mode permanently. This protects you from feeling too much, but it also prevents you from fully living.

The confusion around freeze runs deep. "What's stopping me from acting?" Your nervous system determined freeze was the safest option. "Why am I so numb all the time?" Chronic overwhelm led to chronic shutdown. "Why can't I make myself do things?" Freeze overrides willpower. "Am I just lazy, unmotivated, broken?" No. You're in a biological freeze state.

Freeze served a purpose—it helped you survive impossible situations. The problem isn't that freeze exists; it's that your nervous system hasn't learned that it's safe to come out of freeze now.

EXERCISE: Recognizing Your Freeze Patterns

Section 1 - Acute Freeze Experiences

Think of times when you've felt completely stuck, unable to move or speak. Describe one experience below:

What triggered it?

____

____

____

What did it feel like in your body?

____

____

____

How long did it last?

____

____

What helped you come out of it (if anything)?

____

____

____

Section 2 - Functional Freeze Assessment

Rate each statement: **Never / Sometimes / Often / Always**

I go through daily tasks on autopilot: _______________

I feel emotionally numb or flat most of the time: _______________

I feel disconnected from my body: _______________

Life feels like I'm watching from outside myself: _______________

I struggle to feel joy, even when good things happen: _______________

I feel stuck in my life but can't seem to move forward: _______________

I'm productive but don't feel alive: _______________

I have a sense of being frozen in time: _______________

Reflection

Do I recognize freeze as my nervous system's primary response?

Am I in acute freeze occasionally, or functional freeze chronically?

When did this pattern start?

Functional Freeze and the Illusion of High Performance

Many people with C-PTSD are incredibly high-achieving. They hold demanding jobs, maintain responsibilities, accomplish impressive things. From the outside, they don't look traumatized or stuck. But inside, they feel dead, numb, like they're running on autopilot. How can someone be both frozen and functional?

Functional freeze is accomplishment without presence. The survival part of your brain keeps your body moving through tasks because not doing so would mean vulnerability—losing your job, disappointing people, facing consequences. But the authentic self—the part that feels, connects, experiences joy, makes choices based on desire—is shut down.

You meet deadlines, pay bills, show up to work, but feel like you're operating from outside yourself. You're competent but exhausted because functioning while frozen requires massive energy. You can "perform" socially but feel completely disconnected from the interactions. You achieve things but feel no satisfaction or pride. You make decisions based on "should" instead of genuine desire. You're constantly doing, never being. Success feels empty; accomplishment doesn't register.

High achievers often develop functional freeze for specific reasons. If childhood safety depended on being "good enough," your nervous system learned: "Perform perfectly or face danger." Even when the danger passes, the drive to perform continues—but now it's coming from survival mode, not authentic engagement. Staying busy and achieving keeps you from feeling the pain underneath. As long as you're productive, you don't have to face the emptiness.

If you didn't receive unconditional love in childhood, achievement might have been the only way to receive any positive attention. Now you unconsciously chase external validation because internal worth feels non-existent. Many trauma survivors become the "responsible one"—caretaking others, managing everything, never dropping the ball. This comes from childhood where they had to be parentified or hyper-competent to survive. Functional freeze lets them maintain this role while being emotionally offline.

The suffering of functional freeze is specific. It's invisible, so people don't understand why you're struggling. You feel guilty: "I should be grateful—my life looks good on paper." You can't explain it without sounding ungrateful or privileged. Success doesn't feel like success—you're just surviving in a different way. You're exhausted from maintaining the illusion of okayness.

In functional freeze, there's a split between the part that functions—goes to work, completes tasks, interacts with others—and the part that feels—emotions, desires, authentic self. The functional part keeps operating while the feeling part remains frozen. This split is exhausting to maintain.

Functional freeze is particularly hard to recognize and address because external success makes it seem like "everything is fine." Others might minimize your struggle: "But you're doing so well!" You might dismiss your own pain: "I'm being dramatic—I have it better than most." The freeze is disguised by productivity, so even you don't always recognize it. Thawing from functional freeze doesn't mean becoming less productive. It means reconnecting with your authentic self so that your actions come from choice and engagement, not survival-mode autopilot.

EXERCISE: Functional Freeze Reality Check

External vs. Internal Assessment

From outside, my life looks:

____

____

____

From inside, I feel:

____

____

____

Motivation Assessment

List 5 things you do regularly. For each, mark whether you do it from survival mode (S) or authentic engagement (A):

1. ______________________________ [S / A]
2. ______________________________ [S / A]
3. ______________________________ [S / A]
4. ______________________________ [S / A]
5. ______________________________ [S / A]

Presence Check

When was the last time you felt fully present and engaged (not on autopilot)?

____

____

What percentage of your day do you spend operating from "should" vs. genuine desire?

Should: _______% Genuine desire: _______%

The Core Question

If I could stop performing and just be, what would I feel?

____

____

____

____

____

Thawing Out Through Movement and Sensation

Freeze is a bottom-up problem requiring bottom-up solutions. You can't think your way out of freeze. The parts of the brain that freeze activates are subcortical—they don't respond to logic, willpower, or positive thinking. You have to work through the body.

Movement is the antidote to freeze, but it must be the right kind of movement. Freeze is immobilization, so movement helps complete the interrupted response. But forced or aggressive movement can overwhelm and trigger more shutdown. The movement must be gentle, gradual, and oriented toward pleasure and safety, not achievement.

Phase 1: Reconnecting with Sensation

When deeply frozen, you might not even feel your body. Before you can move out of freeze, you need to reconnect with sensation.

Try a gentle sensing scan. Lie down or sit comfortably. Slowly bring attention to each body part: feet, legs, hands, arms, torso, neck, head. Don't judge what you feel or don't feel. If an area feels numb, just acknowledge: "This area is numb right now." If you feel sensation, describe it neutrally: "warm," "tingling," "tight," "soft."

Explore texture. Hold different textured objects: soft fabric, smooth stone, rough sandpaper, cold ice. Notice how each feels without trying to feel anything specific. This wakes up sensory awareness.

Try temperature awareness. Alternate hot and cold: ice on skin, then warm compress. Notice the difference. Temperature changes can help bring awareness back to the body.

Phase 2: Micro-Movements

Once there's some body awareness, introduce very small movements. Start with finger and toe wiggling. This might feel silly, but for someone in deep freeze, even tiny movement is significant.

Try gentle stretching. Stretch one arm slowly, then the other. Roll shoulders forward, then back. Turn your head slowly side to side. Flex and point your feet.

Rocking can help. Sit in a chair and rock gently forward and back, or lie down and rock side to side. Rhythm is regulating and can help discharge freeze energy.

Self-touch matters. Rub your hands together. Massage your arms, legs, feet. Pat your body gently all over—this is called "tapping in" and helps locate yourself in your body.

Phase 3: Larger Movement

As your system begins to wake up, gradually increase movement. Shaking helps release stuck freeze energy. Stand and shake your body like a dog shaking off water. Start with hands, then arms, then whole body. Let it be messy and uncoordinated.

Pushing activates the fight response in a safe way. Push against a wall with your hands. Feel your muscles engage. Freeze often contains trapped fight and flight energy.

Walking matters, especially outside. Walk slowly at first, paying attention to each step. Notice your feet touching ground. Gradually increase pace as feels comfortable. Walking in nature is particularly helpful.

Dancing reconnects you with your body in a playful way. Move to music however feels good. No rules, no "correct" way.

Yoga or tai chi combine movement, breath, and awareness. Look for trauma-informed yoga classes specifically. The slow, intentional movement helps negotiate thawing.

Phase 4: Completing Interrupted Responses

Peter Levine's Somatic Experiencing approach teaches that freeze often contains incomplete fight or flight responses. Helping your body complete these can release freeze.

Try imaginal completion. Think of a situation where you froze. Imagine what your body wanted to do—run, push away, say no, fight back. In a safe space now, physically do that action: push against a wall as if pushing someone away, run or move quickly as if escaping, say "NO!" or "STOP!" loudly, assume a protective physical posture.

This doesn't change the past, but it helps your nervous system complete the survival response that got interrupted, which can release the freeze.

Critical Guidelines

Go slowly. If you rush, you'll overwhelm your system and trigger more freeze. Slower is faster with trauma work.

Follow pleasure and curiosity, not "should." Move in ways that feel good or interesting, not ways you think you "should" move.

Stop before overwhelm. Work in the stretch zone—slightly uncomfortable but manageable—not the panic zone.

Expect oscillation. Thawing isn't linear. You might feel more alive for a few days, then freeze again. This is normal—your system needs to titrate how much aliveness it can handle.

Be compassionate with yourself. Thawing means feeling more, which includes uncomfortable emotions that were frozen. This is hard. You're not doing it wrong when it's difficult.

EXERCISE: Your Personal Thawing Protocol

Design a simple daily practice for gentle thawing.

Morning (5 minutes) - Choose ONE:

☐ Gentle sensing scan while still in bed

☐ Finger/toe wiggling and stretching

☐ Self-massage of hands, arms, legs

I will do: ____

Midday (2-3 minutes) - Choose ONE:

☐ Walk outside and notice feet touching ground

☐ Push against a wall for 30 seconds

☐ Shake body for 1 minute

I will do: ____

Evening (5-10 minutes) - Choose ONE:

☐ Gentle stretching or yoga

☐ Dance to one song I love

☐ Rock in a chair while breathing slowly

I will do: ____

Weekly Challenge - Pick ONE:

☐ Trauma-informed yoga class

☐ Nature walk focused on sensation

☐ Dance in home for 20 minutes

☐ Practice completing an interrupted response

I will try: ____

After One Week - Reflection:

What did I notice about my body?

____

____

Did I feel more present or alive at any point?

____

____

What movement felt good vs. overwhelming?

____

____

Did I experience oscillation (thawing then re-freezing)?

Reconnecting to Choice When Paralysis Takes Over

Freeze fundamentally disconnects you from your own agency. When frozen, you don't feel like you have choices. Actions feel impossible. Decisions feel overwhelming. You're stuck, and stuckness becomes your identity: "This is just how I am. I can't change. I'm helpless."

This helplessness is both a symptom and a perpetuator of freeze. The freeze state creates helplessness, and believing you're helpless keeps you frozen. Breaking this cycle requires gently reconnecting with the experience of choice, starting microscopically small.

Most advice tells frozen people to make big changes: "Just quit your job!" "Leave that relationship!" "Start that project!" But when you're frozen, even small decisions feel insurmountable. Big changes are completely overwhelming.

Practice the smallest possible choices instead: "Do I want tea or water right now?" "Do I want to wear the blue shirt or the gray one?" "Do I want to sit or stand?" "Do I want to listen to music or silence?"

These choices seem trivial, but they're not—they're your nervous system practicing: "I have some control. I can choose. My preferences matter."

Try this micro-choice practice. Identify something you're about to do on autopilot—make coffee, check phone, start work. Pause and ask: "Do I actually want to do this right now, or am I just doing it because I always do?" If you don't want to, consider an alternative, even for two minutes: "I could wait five minutes before checking my phone" or "I could have tea instead of coffee today." Notice what it feels like to honor your choice, even a tiny one.

The goal isn't to never do things on autopilot—that's impossible. The goal is to interrupt autopilot occasionally and remember you have agency.

"I Don't Know What I Want"

Many freeze-dominant people have disconnected from their desires so long that they genuinely don't know what they want. The question "What do you want?" creates anxiety or blank confusion.

Start with body-based wanting. What does your body want right now? Rest, movement, food, water, warmth, a stretch? Even if you can't feel it clearly, guess and try: "My body might want a stretch." Stretch. Notice if that felt good.

Try the elimination method. "I might not know what I want, but I know I DON'T want ____." Start by identifying what you don't want; what remains is closer to what you might want.

Do a past pleasure audit. Think back to before trauma or early in childhood: what did you enjoy? Those authentic preferences still exist; they're just buried.

Use permission-based questions. Instead of "What do I want?" ask "If I had complete permission to want anything without judgment, what might that be?" This removes the self-criticism that often blocks access to desires.

Reconnecting with "No"

Freeze often originates from situations where "no" wasn't an option. As a result, many frozen people have no access to their "no"—they go along, agree, accommodate, while internally screaming or shutting down.

Reconnecting with "no" is part of thawing. Practice saying no in low-stakes situations. To offers you don't want: "Do you want more food?" "No, thank you." To plans you don't want: "Want to go out Friday?" "No, I'm staying in." To requests that don't work for you: "Can you do this favor?" "No, I'm not available."

Say no to yourself. Notice when you're doing something you don't want to do. Give yourself permission to stop if possible: "I'm going to say no to scrolling social media right now."

Feel what no feels like. When you say no, notice your body. Does it feel relieving? Scary? Powerful? Guilty? The more you practice, the more neutral it becomes.

Rebuilding Decision-Making Capacity

When frozen, even small decisions feel paralyzing. Rebuild this capacity gradually using a decision hierarchy.

Micro decisions: What to eat, wear, when to take a break. Practice these daily.

Small decisions: How to spend free time, what movie to watch. Practice these weekly.

Medium decisions: Changes to routine, new activities, social plans. Approach slowly.

Large decisions: Job changes, relationships, living situations. Only when micro and small decisions feel manageable.

Reduce decision fatigue by creating routines for daily things—same breakfast options, capsule wardrobe. This frees up decision-making capacity for choices that actually matter. Freeze often comes with exhaustion; conserving energy by routinizing trivial decisions helps.

Frozen people often fear making any choice because "What if I choose wrong and something bad happens?" This fear keeps them stuck. Most choices aren't permanent; you can change your mind. "Wrong" choices are how you learn what you actually prefer. The cost of staying frozen—disconnected from life—is higher than the cost of making an imperfect choice. You've survived many difficult things; you can survive making a choice that doesn't work out.

EXERCISE: Daily Agency Practice

Each Day This Week:

Morning: One Body-Based Choice

What does my body want right now?

____

How will I honor that choice today?

____

Midday: One Preference-Based Choice

What am I about to do on autopilot?

____

Do I actually want to do this, or am I just doing it because I always do?

____

Alternative I could try:

____

Evening: One "No" Practice

One small thing I said no to today:

____

What did "no" feel like in my body?

____

End of Day Reflection:

How many times today did I make a conscious choice vs. operate on autopilot?

____

What did it feel like to honor my preferences?

____

Did I notice any resistance to choosing?

____

____

Weekly Challenge:

Make one decision that's slightly bigger than your comfort zone.

What I will try:

☐ Change a routine I usually keep the same

☐ Say yes to something new

☐ Say no to something expected

What happened:

____

____

____

Three Minutes That Could Change Someone's Search

The hardest part about C-PTSD is how invisible it is. You can't show someone your emotional flashbacks or point to your hypervigilance as proof of what you're carrying.

This creates a specific kind of isolation when searching for help. You're trying to figure out if a book will address what you're actually going through or miss it entirely.

When you found this workbook, you probably read reviews first. You were looking for confirmation from people who understood your experience.

Someone is doing that exact search right now.

Your honest review gives them the information they need. Tell them what symptoms you were dealing with. Mention which exercises helped or which concepts finally clicked.

Your review helps:

- One more person recognize their trauma responses aren't character flaws
- One more nervous system begin the process of regulation
- One more life move from survival mode toward actual living

It takes less than 60 seconds. You can leave your review directly from your Amazon purchase page.

I read every review personally. Your feedback, positive or critical, shapes how I develop future resources for C-PTSD recovery.

Thank you for taking the time.

Chapter 7:
Dissociation Is Your Mind's Emergency Exit

"The body says what words cannot." – Martha Graham

You're in a conversation, and suddenly you realize you haven't heard the last few minutes. Your colleague is still talking, their mouth moving, but you have no idea what they just said. You weren't distracted by your phone or thinking about something else. You were just... gone.

Or you drive a familiar route and arrive with no memory of getting there. Your hands turned the wheel, you stopped at lights, you navigated intersections, but you can't recall a single moment of the journey.

Or you look in the mirror and the face looking back doesn't feel like yours. The features are familiar but wrong, like you're looking at a photograph of someone who resembles you but isn't you.

This is dissociation: your mind's emergency exit from overwhelming reality.

Dissociation exists on a spectrum. At one end are experiences everyone has: spacing out during a dull meeting, getting absorbed in a book so completely you don't hear someone calling your name, highway hypnosis on a familiar route. These are normal, temporary disconnections that don't interfere with your life.

At the other end are severe dissociative disorders where identity fragments into separate parts, where memory becomes profoundly unreliable, where reality itself feels questionable. These conditions require intensive professional treatment.

Most people with C-PTSD fall somewhere in the middle. You experience frequent, involuntary disconnection from the present moment, from your body, from your emotions, or from your sense of self. You miss chunks of your life because you weren't there for them. You function, sometimes quite well, but there's always a fog between you and direct experience.

Hypervigilance is too much awareness, scanning constantly for threat. Freeze is immobilization, your body locked in place. Dissociation is different: it's disconnection. Your consciousness exits the situation. Your brain says, "This is too much. I'm taking you offline to protect you."

When you were a child and couldn't physically escape danger, when you couldn't fight an adult or run away from the caregivers you depended on, when freeze became so overwhelming your nervous system needed another option, your mind offered psychological departure. If you couldn't escape the situation, you could escape yourself. You learned to "leave" mentally and emotionally even when physically trapped.

This saved you. A child being screamed at, or hit, or worse, who can mentally transport somewhere else, who can make the present moment feel like it's happening to someone else, experiences less pain. The abuse still damages, but the psychological departure provides a buffer that makes the unbearable slightly more bearable.

The problem is that this emergency exit doesn't close when childhood ends. The dissociative pathways remain active, carved deep into your nervous system. Your brain continues using them not just for overwhelming threats but for any stress, discomfort, or intensity. Difficult conversation with your partner? Exit. Deadline at work? Exit. Someone asks how you're really doing? Exit. Even positive intensity can trigger it: falling in love, achieving something you wanted, feeling genuinely happy. Your system learned that any strong experience is potentially dangerous, so it pulls you out before you can fully feel it.

You've lost control over when you leave and when you stay.

This chapter will help you understand what dissociation is and isn't, recognize your own dissociative patterns, understand why it happens, and learn tools to stay more connected to the present without forcing yourself in ways that feel unsafe. Reconnection is possible, though it requires patience. Your nervous system developed this protection over years, and learning to release it happens gradually, at a pace your system can tolerate.

Dissociation isn't weakness or mental illness. It's an adaptive response that helped you survive unbearable experiences. But living in constant disconnection prevents you from being fully present for your life. You miss the good moments along with the difficult ones. Relationships suffer when people can't reach you. Work becomes harder when you can't concentrate. Time passes, and you can't account for where it went.

Learning to stay grounded when you're safe, and to dissociate less automatically, is part of healing. Not because dissociation is bad, but because you deserve to be present for your own life.

Recognizing When You've Left Your Body

Dissociation can be subtle. Many people with C-PTSD have been dissociating for so long that it feels normal. You don't realize that most people don't spend the majority of their time feeling disconnected from themselves. If you've been gone since childhood, you have no reference point for what presence actually feels like.

Dissociation affects four domains: your body, your emotions, your memory, and your sense of self.

Physical dissociation means your awareness of bodily sensations diminishes or disappears. You don't notice hunger until you're shaky and lightheaded. You don't realize you need to use the bathroom until it's urgent. You push through exhaustion without recognizing you're tired. Physical touch doesn't fully register. Someone hugs you, but you feel it from a distance, muffled and indistinct. You might injure yourself and not realize it until hours later when you see the bruise or cut. Some people describe feeling like they're operating their body remotely, like a pilot flying a plane rather than a person inhabiting their own skin.

You're eating lunch at your desk, but you can't taste it. You're mechanically chewing and swallowing, but there's no sensory experience. The food could be anything.

Emotional dissociation is numbness. Not the heavy sadness of depression, but the complete absence of feeling. You know intellectually that something is sad or joyful, but you can't feel it. You watch a movie that should make you cry, and nothing happens. Someone shares good news, and you smile and say the right things, but inside there's blankness. The emotional volume is turned down to zero. You see feelings happening around you, but they don't reach you.

You want to cry about something that genuinely warrants tears, but when you try, nothing comes. There's just emptiness where feelings should be.

Memory dissociation creates gaps. You lose chunks of time, minutes or hours that you can't account for. You have conversations you don't remember having. You check your text messages and see entire exchanges you don't recall. Your past feels like it happened to someone else, or like a story you heard rather than experiences you lived. The continuity of your life is full of holes, moments that simply aren't there when you try to access them.

Someone references something you said yesterday, and you have no recollection. You search your mind for the memory and find nothing, just blank space where that conversation should be.

Identity dissociation is feeling disconnected from your sense of self. You introduce yourself and your name sounds strange, like you're saying words that don't belong to you. You look in the mirror and the person looking back is familiar but fundamentally wrong, like a copy that's slightly off. You feel like you're made up of different parts that don't fit together. You're one person at work, a different person at home, another person in social situations, and none of them feel like the real you because you're not sure a real you exists.

You're asked to describe yourself, and you realize you have no idea what to say. The question feels impossible, like being asked to describe a color that doesn't exist.

These domains often overlap. You might experience emotional and physical dissociation simultaneously, feeling numb while also disconnected from your body. Or memory dissociation might accompany identity dissociation, where you can't remember parts of your past and also don't feel like that past belongs to you anyway.

Here are moments you might recognize:

You're cooking dinner, following a recipe, but when you're done you can't remember actually making it. The food is there, finished, but the process of creating it is completely absent from your mind.

You're working on your computer, typing, clicking, completing tasks, and suddenly realize you have no idea what you've been doing for the last hour. You were functioning, but you weren't there.

You look down at your hands while you're washing dishes, and they don't look like your hands. They're the wrong size, the wrong shape, alien and unfamiliar, like they belong to someone else and you're borrowing them.

You've been in a meeting for thirty minutes and have zero awareness of what anyone has said. You're sitting there, your eyes are open, you're nodding at appropriate times, but conscious you was completely absent.

You're listening to music you usually love, and it sounds flat, two-dimensional, like it's playing through a broken speaker. The richness is gone. You hear the notes but they don't touch you.

People who've been dissociating since childhood often don't recognize these experiences as dissociation. You might think everyone feels this way, that the distant, low-resolution quality of your experience is just how life is. Or you think you're just "spacey" or "forgetful" or "bad at paying attention" without realizing these are dissociative symptoms.

Dissociation often works with the other C-PTSD symptoms. It pairs with freeze, both dorsal vagal responses that take you offline. It can be triggered by hypervigilance exhaustion: when your system has been on high alert for too long, dissociation offers relief by shutting awareness down. Your nervous system can't maintain maximum vigilance indefinitely, so it swings to the opposite extreme, disconnecting you entirely.

Once you realize how much of your life you've been absent for, it can be frightening. You might panic about how much time you've lost. You might grieve all the moments you missed, all the experiences you were physically present for but not actually there to feel. This reaction makes sense. You're recognizing something significant about how you've moved through the world.

But awareness is the first step toward being more present going forward. You can't change something you don't know is happening. Now you know.

✏ EXERCISE: Your Dissociation Inventory

Rate how often you experienced these in the past week:

Physical Dissociation: Not feeling hunger/pain/exhaustion until extreme • disconnected from body • touch not registering

☐ Rarely ☐ Sometimes ☐ Often ☐ Most of the time

Emotional Dissociation: Feeling numb • unable to access feelings • emotions at a distance

☐ Rarely ☐ Sometimes ☐ Often ☐ Most of the time

Memory Dissociation: Losing time • not remembering conversations • past feeling unreal

☐ Rarely ☐ Sometimes ☐ Often ☐ Most of the time

Identity Dissociation: Disconnected from sense of self • not recognizing yourself • feeling like you're playing a role

☐ Rarely ☐ Sometimes ☐ Often ☐ Most of the time

Which domain is strongest for you? ____

When is dissociation most intense? ____

The Spectrum From Spacing Out to Complete Disconnection

Dissociation isn't one thing. It's not "you either dissociate or you don't." It's dimensional, varying in frequency, intensity, and how many domains it affects.

At the mild end, everyone dissociates sometimes. You daydream during a tedious meeting. You get so absorbed in a book that you don't hear someone calling your name. You drive a familiar route and realize you have no memory of the last few miles because your mind was elsewhere. This is normal and not pathological. It becomes problematic when it's your primary way of relating to life, or when it happens involuntarily in situations where you need to be present.

Moderate dissociation is common in C-PTSD. You're physically present but mentally and emotionally elsewhere most of the time. You lose chunks of time regularly, not just occasionally. Emotional numbness is your baseline, not a temporary state. You experience life at low resolution, details blurred, everything slightly muffled. At this level, dissociation significantly impacts functioning. Relationships suffer because you're not really there when people talk to you. Work becomes harder because you can't concentrate. You miss much of your life because you're absent for it, and the loss accumulates.

Severe dissociation includes significant memory gaps spanning hours or days, feeling like you have distinct parts of yourself that don't communicate, profound confusion about who you are, or experiencing depersonalization and derealization so intense that daily functioning is significantly impaired. Depersonalization is feeling disconnected from yourself: your body doesn't feel like it belongs to you, your voice sounds strange and distant when you speak, you observe your actions as if you're a character being controlled rather than a person making choices. Derealization is feeling like the world around you isn't real: everything looks flat and two-dimensional, objects and people seem distant or dreamlike, nothing feels solid or substantial.

In extreme cases, this level becomes disorders like Dissociative Identity Disorder, where the personality fragments into distinct parts with separate memories and ways of being, or Depersonalization/Derealization Disorder, where chronic unreality becomes the constant state. These conditions need professional treatment beyond what self-help can provide.

Most dissociation in C-PTSD falls into the moderate range, though it can spike into severe during high stress or when triggered.

Different types of dissociative experiences exist within this spectrum:

Emotional numbing is complete absence of feeling. Not sadness, which is a feeling, but absolute flatness. You know intellectually that something should make you happy or sad, but there's zero emotional response inside. This often accompanies freeze, your system protecting you from overwhelming affect by shutting it down entirely.

Time distortion makes time move too fast, too slow, or lose meaning altogether. Hours pass in what feels like minutes, or minutes stretch into what feels like hours. You lose sense of linear time. Past, present, and future blur together. You might be unsure what day it is or how much time has passed since something happened.

Compartmentalization keeps different parts of your life or self completely separate, to the point where they don't feel connected. Work-you and home-you feel like different people who don't share information. Traumatized-you and functional-you exist in separate compartments that never interact. This allows you to function in daily life by keeping trauma memories and feelings sealed off, but it also means you're never whole. The parts don't integrate.

Structural dissociation is a concept from trauma theory describing how the personality can split into parts: one focused on daily functioning, one holding trauma, sometimes many more. This isn't the same as DID, but it describes how trauma can fragment the sense of self into distinct parts that don't always communicate. You might have a part that goes to work and manages responsibilities, a part that holds terror and rage from childhood, a part that tries to soothe and take care of everyone, and these parts might not feel like they're all you. They feel like separate entities operating the same body.

The severity of dissociation generally correlates with trauma severity and timing. The earlier trauma began, the longer it lasted, and the more inescapable it was, the more severe the dissociation tends to be. Trauma before age five, when identity is still forming, is most likely to cause significant structural dissociation. The child's developing sense of self fractures under the weight of what's happening, creating separate compartments to contain the unbearable. But even trauma later in childhood or adolescence can cause problematic dissociation if it was severe enough or lasted long enough.

Different intensities of dissociation serve different functions. Mild dissociation helps you get through boring or mildly stressful situations without feeling every minute. Moderate dissociation helped you survive ongoing trauma by keeping you disconnected from unbearable pain. Severe dissociation developed when trauma was so overwhelming that fragmenting was the only way to contain it. By keeping traumatic experiences in one "part" while another part could function in daily life, you could go to school, interact with people, complete tasks, even though something terrible was happening or had happened to you.

Dissociation intensity fluctuates. You might be moderately dissociated most of the time but experience severe dissociation when triggered. Or you might have periods of relative presence followed by periods of deep disconnection. Trauma anniversaries intensify dissociation, even when you're not consciously aware of the date. Stress makes it worse. Relationship conflicts, work pressure, or anything that echoes original trauma can deepen disconnection. Sometimes there's no identifiable trigger, and you just wake up one day feeling more absent than usual.

EXERCISE: Mapping Your Dissociation Spectrum

Frequency:

☐ Rarely
☐ Weekly
☐ Daily
☐ Most waking hours

Intensity:

☐ Mild spacing out
☐ Moderate disconnection
☐ Severe unreality

Types (check all that apply):

☐ Depersonalization
☐ Derealization
☐ Emotional numbing
☐ Time loss
☐ Memory gaps
☐ Identity confusion
☐ Compartmentalization

What intensifies it?

☐ Stress
☐ Conflict
☐ Intimacy
☐ Success
☐ Specific people
☐ Trauma reminders
☐ No identifiable trigger

Impact (0-10): Relationships ____ Work ____ Daily life ____ Overall quality ____

Where do you fall? ☐ Mild ☐ Moderate ☐ Severe

Has this changed over time? ☐ Better ☐ Worse ☐ Same

Grounding Techniques That Actually Work

Grounding techniques bring your awareness back to the present moment, back into your body, and back to external reality. They counter dissociation by engaging your senses, activating your thinking brain, and reminding your nervous system where and when you actually are.

For dissociation, standard grounding techniques often need to be more intense than what works for anxiety or mild stress. When you're disconnected, your sensory awareness is dampened. You need stronger signals to break through: sharper temperatures, more powerful smells, bolder flavors, clearer physical sensations. Gentle techniques might not register at all.

The key is practicing when you're calm, not just in crisis. If you only try grounding techniques when you're severely dissociated, your brain doesn't know how to use them. The neural pathways aren't established. Practice when you're mildly disconnected or even when you're relatively present, so the techniques become familiar and accessible when you need them most.

Different senses work better for different people. Your job is finding what works for your nervous system.

Physical grounding through temperature is often most effective for dissociation. Hold ice cubes until they melt completely in your hands. The cold and slight pain are intensely grounding. Run your hands under very cold water, then very hot water, focusing entirely on the temperature shift. Take a cold shower. Press an ice pack to your neck or face. Temperature extremes break through numbness faster than almost anything else.

Tactile grounding with strong textures brings immediate body awareness. Carry a grounding object: something rough like sandpaper, something with sharp edges like a ridged stone, something soft but heavy like a fabric pouch filled with rice. When dissociated, hold it and focus entirely on how it feels. Press your feet firmly into the ground and notice the pressure moving through your legs. Touch different surfaces and name them aloud, emphasizing extreme contrasts: "Cold metal. Warm wood. Rough concrete."

Olfactory grounding works because smell connects directly to memory and emotion centers in your brain, shifting states rapidly. For dissociation, use the strongest scents you can find: peppermint oil (put a drop on your wrist and smell it), coffee grounds held directly under your nose, fresh citrus peel squeezed to release oils, eucalyptus. Ammonia inhalants work for severe dissociation but use them carefully. Carry a small vial of essential oil dedicated to grounding. When dissociated, smell it repeatedly until your awareness sharpens.

Gustatory grounding with intense flavors pulls you back into your body. Keep sour candy (the more sour the better), strong mints, crystallized ginger, or hot sauce accessible. When you feel yourself disappearing, put something intensely flavored in your mouth and focus completely on the taste. Chew on a whole peppercorn or a piece of raw ginger. The stronger and more unexpected the flavor, the more it grounds you.

Movement-based grounding forces body awareness through action. Stomp your feet hard, feeling the impact reverberate through your legs. Jump up and down twenty times. Do ten jumping jacks, counting each one aloud. Sprint up stairs. The physical exertion combined with counting creates dual focus that breaks dissociation. For some people, exercise is their primary grounding tool: the sustained physical demand makes it impossible to stay disconnected.

Reality orientation for dissociation specifically targets the gaps dissociation creates. Say aloud: "My name is [name]. I am [age] years old. Today is [day, date, year]. I am in [specific location]. The time is [check clock and say it]. I am safe right now." Touch the wall or floor while you say this. The combination of speaking, hearing your voice, touching something solid, and anchoring to specific facts counteracts unreality. If you're losing time, set hourly alarms and each time one goes off, orient yourself: say the time, where you are, what you're doing.

Cognitive grounding for severe dissociation engages your prefrontal cortex with tasks demanding focused attention. Count backwards from 100 by sevens. Name every state alphabetically, then countries, then cities. Describe the room you're in to an imaginary person, including every detail. Solve mental math problems. The cognitive demand pulls your brain back online and makes dissociation harder to maintain.

Visual detail work grounds through observation. Pick one object and describe it exhaustively for sixty seconds: color, texture, shadows, reflections, imperfections. Or do a room inventory: name and describe fifteen separate objects you can see. The level of detail matters more than what you're looking at. Forcing yourself to notice specifics activates observation rather than absence.

If you're losing large chunks of time, address time awareness specifically. Wear a watch and check it regularly. Set reminders every hour that say "Where are you? What are you doing?" Keep a small notebook and write the time and location every time you change activities. This creates external structure when internal time sense fails.

If standard grounding doesn't work, don't assume you're doing it wrong. Some people are so deeply dissociated that they need multiple techniques simultaneously: hold ice while smelling peppermint oil while counting backwards. Or you might need to address what's causing the dissociation. If you're disconnecting to escape overwhelming emotions, grounding alone might not work until you address the emotions with support.

The difference between forcing yourself to be present and inviting yourself to be present matters. Grounding should feel like bringing yourself back, not punishing yourself for leaving. If grounding creates more panic or discomfort, back off. Dissociation is protecting you from something. Forcing presence before your system feels safe enough can be retraumatizing. Sometimes your nervous system still needs the exit.

EXERCISE: Building Your Personal Grounding Menu

Try one technique from each category this week. Rate effectiveness (1-10).

Temperature: ______________________________________ Rating: ____

Strong texture: ______________________________________ Rating: ____

Intense smell: ______________________________________ Rating: ____

Bold flavor: ______________________________________ Rating: ____

Movement: ______________________________________ Rating: ____

Reality orientation: ______________________________________ Rating: ____

My three most effective techniques:

1. ____
2. ____
3. ____

What I need to keep accessible:

____

____

Staying Present Without Forcing Yourself

You want to be present, but presence feels threatening. When you start to ground and come back into your body, anxiety spikes. Overwhelming emotions surface. Your chest tightens, your breathing gets shallow, and you instinctively dissociate again because presence doesn't feel safe.

Your system learned that being present means being vulnerable to pain. Dissociation became protection. Learning to stay present requires building tolerance gradually and creating enough safety that your nervous system no longer needs constant escape.

The goal isn't eliminating dissociation. It's recovering choice about when you use your emergency exit. Can you stay present when you're safe? Can you choose to disconnect temporarily when you need relief, then choose to come back? This is different from reducing freeze or managing hypervigilance, where the aim is decreasing the response itself. With dissociation, you're learning to toggle the exit consciously rather than having it slam shut or stay permanently open without your input.

You don't have to go from completely dissociated to fully present in one step. Practice being incrementally more present, in doses your system can handle.

Pendulation comes from Somatic Experiencing. Instead of trying to stay grounded continuously, which can overwhelm your nervous system, practice moving between presence and disconnection intentionally. Ground yourself for thirty seconds, noticing what presence feels like. Then allow yourself to dissociate for thirty seconds, giving yourself explicit permission to leave. Then ground again. Then allow disconnection. This back-and-forth teaches your system that presence is tolerable because it's not permanent. You're practicing that you can approach and withdraw, come back and go away, without losing control of the toggle. Over time, the periods of presence can lengthen naturally because your system knows the exit is still available.

What often drives dissociation is that body sensations or emotions are overwhelming. Practice staying with sensation in very small doses. Notice a body sensation: tension in your shoulders, tightness in your chest, warmth in your hands. Stay with it for five seconds. Then distract yourself or let yourself dissociate if needed. Gradually increase to ten seconds, twenty seconds, thirty seconds. You're building capacity to feel without being flooded. The specific skill here is tolerating increasing durations of sensory awareness, which is different from learning to stay in freeze long enough to thaw, or managing the intensity of emotions like shame. You're measuring presence in seconds and minutes, tracking how long you can stay before you need to use the exit.

The container technique helps when emotions or memories drive your dissociation. Visualize a container where you can safely put difficult emotions or memories: a box, a vault, a chest with a lock. Tell yourself, "I acknowledge this is here, and I'm putting it in the container for now. I'll address it later when I have support." This allows you to be present now without being overwhelmed by what you're protecting yourself from. This isn't avoidance. It's controlled, intentional postponement so you can function in the moment.

Your nervous system dissociates when it doesn't feel safe to be present. Build environmental and relational safety cues. Identify safe spaces where you practice presence. Identify safe people whose presence doesn't require dissociation. Use objects or images that signal safety to you. The more safety cues you have, the less your system needs to dissociate.

Some trauma survivors dissociate not just from pain but from positive intensity: joy, excitement, connection, pleasure. These feelings became dangerous in childhood. Either because good things didn't last and the loss hurt more than never having them, or because showing happiness led to punishment or mockery, or because feeling good left you vulnerable. If you dissociate from positive experiences, practice staying present for brief moments of pleasure. Notice something that feels good for five seconds. Don't force it longer. Gradually increase. Teach your system that aliveness isn't dangerous.

Co-regulation helps. Being with someone who's present and calm can help you stay present without feeling overwhelmed. This doesn't mean you're dependent on others. It means you're using relational resources to build your own capacity. Over time, you internalize this. The calm presence you borrow from others becomes something you can access within yourself.

Some moments are genuinely too overwhelming to be fully present for. Medical procedures. Trauma therapy processing. Acute grief. Give yourself permission to dissociate when needed. Intentional, temporary disconnection as a coping tool is different from chronic, involuntary dissociation as your only state. You're learning to operate the emergency exit deliberately rather than having it stuck open or triggered automatically by anything intense.

Progress doesn't mean you're suddenly present all the time. It means you notice when you dissociate. You can sometimes choose to ground. You can tolerate being present for slightly longer periods. The dissociation happens less frequently or less intensely. These incremental shifts matter more than complete transformation. You're building a skill, and skills develop gradually through practice.

When you've dissociated through much of your life, becoming more present means realizing how much you missed. You might grieve the years you were absent for: the relationships you were only half-there for, the experiences you went through but didn't fully feel, the person you might have been if you'd been able to stay. This grief is valid. Being present now doesn't erase that loss, but it prevents you from losing more time.

EXERCISE: Practicing Titrated Presence

Daily practice (5-10 minutes):

1. **Ground (30 sec):** Use your strongest grounding technique.

What does presence feel like? ____

2. **Stay with sensation (10 sec):** Pick one body sensation and notice it.

3. **Permission to dissociate (30 sec):** Allow yourself to space out.

4. **Return (30 sec):** Ground again.

Repeat 2-3 times.

After one week:

How long can you stay present? _______ seconds

What helps you tolerate presence? ____

Weekly challenge: Choose one activity you typically do dissociated:

☐ Showering ☐ Eating ☐ Commuting ☐ Other: ____________________

Practice being present for the first 60 seconds.

What did you notice? ____

Chapter 8:
The Anger and Rage You've Been Hiding

"Anger is meant to be acted upon. It is not meant to be acted out." — Julia Cameron

Your jaw locks when someone speaks to you in that tone. Your chest tightens like something is being compressed inside a container too small to hold it. You imagine slamming doors inside yourself—violent, satisfying—but your face stays neutral. Or there's nothing. You search for anger about what happened to you and find only a vast, careful emptiness where the feeling should be.

Anger is the emotion trauma survivors fear most. Fear makes sense after trauma. Sadness is understandable. But anger? Anger felt radioactive in your childhood home—something that contaminated everything it touched. You learned not to get near it. Anger made the abuse worse. Anger proved you were difficult, ungrateful, out of control. Your survival depended on keeping anger locked away, so you learned to compress it into something smaller, redirect it at yourself, or go completely blank whenever it threatened to surface.

You didn't just learn that expressing anger was dangerous. You learned that feeling it meant you were dangerous. The people who hurt you used their anger as a weapon, so you concluded that anger itself was the weapon. The thought became automatic: if I let myself feel this, I become toxic. I become what hurt me. This belief runs deeper than logic. It's written in your nervous system.

Trauma survivors have distinct patterns with anger. Some compress it so tightly it becomes a dense, hidden mass that affects everything without ever being visible. Some experience sudden eruptions where years of accumulated rage break through over something small. Some direct anger only at themselves or people who can't retaliate while staying silent with those who actually violated them. Some have disconnected from anger so completely they describe themselves as "not an angry person" while their bodies tell a different story—chronic pain, jaw tension, digestive problems.

This chapter will show you why anger was compressed, the physical and psychological cost of anger that has nowhere to go, the difference between healthy anger and destructive rage, and methods for creating safe channels where anger can discharge without harming you or others.

Your anger is valid. It's information about how you were treated and what you deserve now. Learning to work with anger doesn't make you toxic—compressing it or erupting it does. Healthy anger is a resource for healing, boundary-setting, and reclaiming your life.

Why Fear Feels Safer Than Fury

You learned early that anger was dangerous to express. Children are powerless against adults. Showing anger at an abusive or neglectful caregiver didn't improve anything—it escalated danger. Anger led to worse abuse, punishment, rejection, abandonment. The lesson became cellular: expressing anger threatens survival.

The safer strategy became fear. Stay scared, stay vigilant, stay compliant. Fear kept you small and unthreatening. Fear didn't provoke retaliation. So the anger that should have been directed outward—at the people harming you—got compressed, and fear became the only emotion you were allowed to inhabit.

Both anger and fear activate your sympathetic nervous system, but the child experiencing abuse can't fight back (too small, too dependent) and can't flee (nowhere to go). The anger—the fight response—didn't get frozen like trauma responses often do. It got compacted. Like you were trying to compress an explosion into a container too small to hold it. The energy didn't disappear. It got denser, harder, more concentrated inside you.

Many trauma survivors develop what amounts to a phobia of their own rage. Not because they fear losing control in an abstract sense, but because they witnessed what anger could do when someone else used it as a weapon. The anger itself seemed like the problem. You couldn't distinguish between the feeling and how your abuser weaponized it, so you concluded that all anger was contaminating.

When anger can't be expressed outward, it doesn't disappear. It stratifies.

You turn it inward as self-hatred. The anger that should be directed at those who harmed you gets directed at yourself. You become your own target. This shows up as harsh self-criticism, self-sabotage, self-harm. It's safer to be angry at yourself than at powerful others. You can't be abandoned by yourself.

Or anger converts to depression. The energy of anger, when compressed over years, becomes the flatness and weight of depression. You don't feel rage—you feel hopeless, exhausted. The anger is still there, but it's been compacted into something that feels less threatening to others.

Some people express anger through their bodies instead of their voices. Chronic tension headaches. Jaw pain from clenching teeth at night. Digestive issues that flare when you're around certain people. Doing too much—hyper-responsibility as a way of channeling the energy into "acceptable" productivity. Your body becomes the pressure valve when your voice can't be.

Or you displace anger onto safe targets. You can't be angry at your abusive parent or demanding boss, so you snap at your partner over something trivial. The anger finds an outlet, but not the right one. This creates guilt and damages relationships, which then reinforces the belief that your anger is destructive.

Some trauma survivors disconnect from anger so thoroughly they genuinely don't feel it. They describe themselves as "never angry." The anger is there—underneath the careful blankness—but accessing it feels impossible. You didn't separate from the world. You separated from the volcano inside yourself.

Chronically compressed anger doesn't just stay quietly contained. It causes physical problems—chronic pain, autoimmune conditions, high blood pressure, TMJ. It causes psychological problems—

depression, anxiety, self-hatred. It causes relational problems—resentment stratifies in layers, boundaries fail, authentic connection becomes impossible because you can't be honest about what you feel.

Fear feels safer than anger because feeling scared confirmed the role that was assigned to you. You were supposed to be small, compliant, grateful. Fear maintained that position. Anger threatened the entire family system. Anger said: something here is wrong. That acknowledgment was too dangerous when your survival depended on keeping the system stable, even if the system was harming you.

✏ EXERCISE: Tracking Your Suppressed Anger

Childhood Messages

What happened when you expressed anger as a child?

____

____

Current Patterns (check what applies)

☐ I never feel angry

☐ I'm angry at myself more than others

☐ I get angry at safe people, silent with those who harmed me

☐ I feel depressed or numb often

☐ My body holds tension (jaw, shoulders, stomach)

☐ I do too much, stay busy to avoid feeling

What You Feel Instead of Anger

When something happens that should make you angry, you feel:

☐ Fear ☐ Shame ☐ Numbness ☐ Self-blame ☐ Physical pain

What You Believe

If I fully feel and express my anger:

____

____

____

Discovering the Protective Power of Healthy Anger

Healthy anger and destructive rage are not the same thing.

Healthy anger is clear, boundaried, proportional, and protective. It says: this is not okay. You're crossing a line. I need this to change. Healthy anger mobilizes self-protection without destroying. It can be expressed firmly without cruelty. It defends without attacking. It sets boundaries without violating others' boundaries.

Destructive rage is uncontrolled, explosive, disproportionate, and harmful. It seeks to hurt, punish, or destroy. It's anger without boundaries—it doesn't stop at protection but goes into attack. It's the anger that traumatized you—the anger you witnessed from your abuser.

Healthy anger is not what hurt you. Destructive rage is what hurt you. Learning to access healthy anger doesn't make you toxic. Your abuser's problem wasn't that they felt anger—it was that they used it as a weapon against people with less power. That's the difference. Power differential plus uncontrolled rage equals abuse. Healthy anger respects boundaries and doesn't target the vulnerable.

Healthy anger serves specific protective functions.

Anger signals violations through your body before your mind catches up. A microspasm in your shoulders when someone dismisses you. Your jaw tightening when someone speaks to you in a condescending tone. A subtle lean away from someone who just crossed a line. These physical signals happen before you consciously think "that's not okay." If you've learned to ignore these signals, you can't protect yourself effectively.

Anger mobilizes action. Fear immobilizes—it makes you freeze or flee. Anger mobilizes—it gives you energy to say no, to leave, to defend yourself, to change a situation. Without anger, you stay stuck in situations that harm you because you lack the energy to change them.

Anger validates your worth. When you feel angry about mistreatment, you're implicitly acknowledging: I deserve better than this. Anger requires you to believe you're worthy of respect. Compressing anger often goes hand-in-hand with believing you don't deserve better.

Anger completes interrupted responses. Trauma often involves situations where you couldn't fight back or defend yourself. That fight energy didn't get frozen—it got interrupted mid-process. The anger you should have felt then got locked away. Expressing anger now can help complete that interrupted response, finishing what your nervous system couldn't finish when you were powerless.

Many trauma survivors don't feel angry about their abuse while it's happening or immediately after—they feel fear, shame, or blankness. The anger comes later, sometimes years or decades later. This isn't delayed processing in the way trauma memories are delayed. It's reactivation of a process that was interrupted. Your system is finally allowing the interrupted response to complete. If you're feeling rage now about something that happened years ago, your body is trying to finish something it couldn't finish then.

You can feel rageful without acting rageful. You can acknowledge furious thoughts without expressing them to the person you're furious with. Part of healthy anger is having the internal experience fully while choosing conscious, boundaried external expression. You're not compressing the anger—you're feeling it completely while choosing how to express it appropriately.

Anger is information. It tells you something needs attention. "I'm angry that I've controlled myself for years to keep others comfortable" might mean "I need to stop prioritizing others' comfort over my own needs." "I'm angry at my body for not being different" might mean "I need to grieve what was taken from me." The anger itself isn't the problem to eliminate—it's data pointing you toward what needs to change.

Accessing anger after years of compression can feel uncomfortable at first. You might worry you're becoming contaminated by it. You might feel guilty for feeling angry at people you love. You might fear you're becoming what hurt you. These are normal responses when you've spent your life keeping anger contained. You're not becoming an angry person—you're becoming a person who has access to all your emotions, including anger.

EXERCISE: Reframing Your Relationship With Anger

Old Belief → New Understanding

Complete these reframes:

"Anger is toxic" → ______________________________

"If I'm angry, I'm contaminated" → ______________________________

"My anger will destroy everything" → ______________________________

Anger as Information

Think of a situation where you should feel angry but don't.

What happened: ______________________________

If you gave yourself permission to be angry, what would it tell you?

____

What did you deserve that you didn't get?

____

Permission Statement

I am angry that ______________________________

because I deserved ____

Expressing Rage Without Destroying Yourself or Others

If you've been compressing anger for years or decades, when it finally surfaces, it can feel enormous—volcanic, terrifying, uncontrollable. This intensity doesn't mean you're dangerous. It means you have years of accumulated anger that needs safe channels for discharge. The goal isn't to make the anger smaller or more acceptable—it's to create pathways where it can decompress without causing harm.

Compressing anger keeps it locked in your body, causing physical and psychological damage. Erupting anger outward harms relationships and confirms your fear that you're toxic. The third option is creating deliberate decompression channels—expressing anger fully in contexts where it won't damage you or others.

Think of these as anger rituals—designated times and spaces where you give yourself full permission to let the pressure release.

Physical Decompression Methods

These work because anger is compressed energy that needs physical pathways out.

Pillow or mattress hitting creates a channel for discharge. Take a pillow or use your mattress. Hit it, punch it, throw it. Let yourself make noise—yell, scream, growl. Continue until the pressure feels released. Your body doesn't distinguish between hitting a person and hitting a pillow—the decompression happens either way.

Tearing and ripping satisfies the destructive impulse without causing actual harm. Tear up old phone books, newspapers, cardboard boxes. The physical act of destroying something releases the energy. Some people keep a "rage box" filled with paper specifically for this. When pressure builds, they tear.

Ice throwing combines impact with sound. Go outside and throw ice cubes at the ground or against a wall as hard as you can. The sound of shattering creates satisfaction. The ice melts—nothing permanently broken, but the energy is released through the act.

Exercise intensity channels compressed energy into movement. Run hard, hit a punching bag, do intense cardio, lift heavy weights. Your body uses the same pathways for anger discharge and intense physical exertion.

Screaming releases pressure from your throat—where unexpressed words compress. Scream in your car with the windows up, into a pillow, or in a place where you won't be heard. Let yourself scream from your gut—not words, just sound. Feel the vibration move through your chest and throat. This creates an internal pathway for release.

Controlled breaking can decompress years of compressed rage when done safely. Some cities have rage rooms. Or create your own version—buy cheap dishes from a thrift store and break them outside in a garbage bag with safety glasses. The act of breaking something intentionally creates a safe channel for destructive energy.

Vocal Decompression Methods

Much of compressed anger lives in your throat—words you weren't allowed to say.

Impulsive letter writing lets you discharge without consequences. Write letters to people you're angry at. Don't think, don't edit, don't make it coherent—just let the raw anger pour onto paper. Curse, rage, say everything you've never been able to say. You will not send these. Burn them or tear them up. The point is creating an exit channel.

Rage journaling is rapid, broken, unfiltered. Set a timer for ten minutes and write every angry thought without lifting the pen. No punctuation, no structure, no concern for making sense. Write so fast your hand cramps. This externalizes compressed anger instead of leaving it trapped inside.

Speaking to an empty chair creates a focal point for confrontation. When alone, speak your anger to an empty chair. Imagine the person you're angry at sitting there and tell them everything. This is confrontation practice, not reflection. Yell if you need to. Let your voice be as loud as the pressure inside.

Recording yourself provides both release and witness. Record your angry rants on your phone. You can play it back later or delete it immediately—either way, you've externalized the compressed energy.

Creative Decompression Methods

For those who feel too unsafe to express anger directly, creative channels provide distance.

Art lets you discharge visually. Paint or draw your anger. Use aggressive strokes, dark colors, chaotic images. Don't worry about it being good—let it be pure discharge. Slash paint across canvas. Create images of destruction.

Music provides anger you can embody. Listen to angry music and move to it. Or play an instrument aggressively—drums are particularly effective for discharge. Singing along to angry songs lets you channel rage through someone else's words.

Writing fiction allows discharge through characters. Create characters who express the rage you can't. Write scenes where they say what you wish you could say, do what you wish you could do. This provides distance while allowing full discharge.

Movement lets your body decompress. Put on intense music and move however your anger wants to move—stomping, punching the air, aggressive dancing. Move until the pressure releases.

Imaginal Decompression

When you can't physically confront the person who harmed you—they're absent, dead, or unsafe to confront—imagination creates a container.

Visualization creates a safe space for confrontation. Close your eyes. Visualize the person who harmed you. Tell them everything you need to say. Imagine yourself powerful and them unable to retaliate. This stays in your imagination—safe and contained but still allowing full discharge.

The empty chair technique gives compressed anger a physical focus. Put an empty chair in front of you. Imagine the person who hurt you sitting there. Confront them. Let yourself be as angry as you need to be. The chair provides a focal point without requiring the actual person.

Guidelines for Safe Decompression

Do this alone or with a therapist. Don't discharge unprocessed rage at actual people. Dumping compressed rage on others—even those who deserve your anger—isn't healthy expression. It's reactive eruption.

Set time boundaries. Set a timer—twenty to thirty minutes. This prevents getting stuck in rage and ensures you have time to ground afterward.

Ground yourself afterward. After decompression work, drink water, breathe deeply, splash cold water on your face. You've opened decompression channels—now help your system settle.

Don't judge yourself. If you feel ridiculous hitting a pillow or guilty for feeling rage toward someone you also love, notice the judgment but do the practice anyway.

Track what helps. Some people find physical decompression cathartic. Others find it amplifies pressure. Pay attention to how you feel afterward. Your system will tell you what works.

You're not creating more anger. You're decompressing what's been accumulated for years. Most people find that after consistently using safe channels, the intensity decreases over time. Once it's discharged, there's less pressure.

EXERCISE: Your Anger Decompression Practice

This Week, Try:

Choose two methods:

Physical: ☐ Pillow hitting ☐ Ice throwing ☐ Exercise ☐ Tearing paper

Vocal: ☐ Impulsive letter ☐ Rage journaling ☐ Empty chair ☐ Screaming

Creative: ☐ Angry art ☐ Music ☐ Movement ☐ Writing

Track:

Method 1: ________________________

Before (0-10): _____ After (0-10): _____

Method 2: ________________________

Before (0-10): ____ After (0-10): ____

Which felt most effective?

____

Commit to Weekly Practice:

I will practice ______________________ once a week.

____

Transforming Anger Into Boundary-Setting Fuel

Anger arises when boundaries are violated. If you don't feel anger when someone crosses your boundaries, you probably won't set boundaries effectively. If you feel anger but don't use it to inform boundary-setting, the anger stays compressed and either implodes or erupts.

Healthy anger doesn't need to be expressed as anger externally—it can be translated into calm, firm boundary-setting. You feel the full fury internally, but what comes out is clear, non-aggressive assertion: "That doesn't work for me." "I need you to stop." "I'm not available for that." The anger fuels the boundary without being the form the boundary takes.

Anger brings alignment. When you're angry, something inside you straightens. Your mind stops producing fog. Your body knows with certainty what's not acceptable. The confusion and people-pleasing that normally cloud your thinking disappear. Your chest opens. Your breath stabilizes. Use that alignment to identify what boundary needs to be set.

The Anger-to-Boundary Process

Step 1: Feel the anger fully (privately)

Before setting a boundary, feel the anger completely. Don't compress it to be "nice." Feel the rage, acknowledge what was violated, validate that you deserve better. Use decompression methods if needed. You need the full power of the anger to fuel the boundary.

Step 2: Identify what the anger is protecting

Anger always protects something—your dignity, your time, your safety. Ask: What is this anger protecting? What do I need that I'm not getting? The answer becomes your boundary.

Step 3: Translate into boundary statement

The anger becomes: "I need [X]" or "I'm not available for [Y]" or "[Z] is not okay with me." The statement is firm but not hostile. You're not attacking—you're protecting.

Step 4: Communicate the boundary clearly

State what you need or what's not acceptable. You don't have to explain or justify. Boundaries are about your limits, not negotiation.

Step 5: Follow through

Boundaries without enforcement aren't boundaries—they're suggestions. If someone crosses the boundary again, there must be a consequence. Your anger gives you the energy to follow through.

Examples of Translating Anger Into Boundaries

Anger: "I'm furious that I've organized my entire life around managing others' emotions."

Boundary: "I'm no longer available to manage how you feel about my choices. You can be upset, and I can still make decisions that work for me."

Anger: "I'm enraged at how I've withdrawn from everything to avoid conflict."

Boundary (internal): "I'm not shrinking myself anymore to keep situations comfortable. If my presence creates discomfort, that's information, not my responsibility."

Anger: "I'm angry that my partner dismisses what I say when I try to talk about something that hurt me."

Boundary: "When I share something that hurt me, I need it to be heard. If you can't do that right now, I'll end the conversation and we can revisit it when you're able to listen."

Anger: "I'm furious at decades of compressing myself."

Boundary (internal): "I'm creating limits to contain the combustion inside. No more working past exhaustion. No more saying yes when I mean no. These boundaries aren't for others—they're to keep me from burning out from the inside."

Assertive vs. Aggressive Communication

Aggressive communication comes from compressed rage erupting: "You're so selfish! You never think about anyone else!" This attacks, uses absolutes, escalates conflict.

Assertive communication comes from anger channeled into protection. Your chest is open. Your breath is stable. Your jaw is relaxed. You speak from alignment, not attack: "When you cancel plans last-minute, I feel disrespected. I'm not willing to continue this pattern. I need reliability."

The anger is fully present in the assertive version—it's what gives you the energy to speak—but it's channeled into clear communication instead of eruption.

Protective vs. Punitive Anger

Protective anger says: "I'm drawing a line to keep myself safe." Punitive anger says: "I'm going to make you suffer." Protective anger sets boundaries. Punitive anger seeks revenge. The former moves you forward. The latter keeps you stuck.

When setting boundaries, check your motivation. Are you protecting yourself or punishing them? Protection is about your safety now. Punishment is about making them hurt. Protection is necessary. Punishment is optional and often counterproductive.

Boundaries With People Who Harmed You

Sometimes the anger is about old violations. You can't retroactively set boundaries for the past, but you can protect yourself now. "I'm no longer available for conversations that involve criticism of my choices." "If you bring up [topic], I'll end the call." "I'm limiting contact to [specific frequency] or no contact."

These boundaries protect your current self. They shift focus from what they did then to what you need now.

Self-Boundaries to Contain Internal Combustion

Sometimes your anger is at yourself for patterns you keep repeating. This anger can fuel self-boundaries—limits to contain the combustion inside before it burns you out. "I'm not working past exhaustion anymore." "I'm not spending time with people who drain me just because I feel obligated." "I'm not compressing myself to keep situations comfortable."

These aren't promises or goals. They're containment structures fueled by the anger at what self-abandonment has cost you.

Boundary-setting gets easier with practice. The first boundary will feel terrifying. Your nervous system will signal danger. The guilt will be overwhelming. That's normal—you're doing something you were never allowed to do. It gets easier. Your anger will continue to fuel your boundaries until protecting yourself feels normal instead of dangerous.

EXERCISE: From Anger to Boundaries

Identify Your Anger

What are you angry about right now?

____

What's Being Violated?

What do you deserve that you're not getting?

____

Craft Your Boundary

"I need ____"

or

"I'm not available for ____"

Practice

Say it out loud three times.

Where do you feel resistance? ______________________________________

Where do you feel alignment? ______________________________________

Challenge

Set one boundary this week:

What: ____

With whom: ____

When: ____

Chapter 9:
Self-Compassion When You've Never Known Kindness

"You yourself, as much as anybody in the entire universe, deserve your love and affection." — Sharon Salzberg

Try saying something kind to yourself right now. Go ahead. "I'm doing my best." "This is hard, and that's okay." "I deserve rest."

Notice what happens in your body. Does your chest tighten? Does your throat close? Do you physically cringe, like you've said something embarrassing? Does a wave of nausea or discomfort move through you? This isn't resistance in your thoughts. It's your body rejecting kindness like a transplanted organ that doesn't recognize the donor.

For people who grew up with C-PTSD, self-compassion produces a physical recoil. Your nervous system has no template for it. You've heard the advice a thousand times: "be kinder to yourself." Nobody explained that kindness would feel this foreign in your body, this awkward in your mouth, this fundamentally wrong.

The problem isn't that you don't understand self-compassion conceptually. You can explain it perfectly: treat yourself with the understanding you'd offer others, acknowledge your humanity, be gentle with your struggles. You know what it means. You just have no embodied experience of receiving it. When compassion never entered your nervous system from the outside, generating it from the inside feels like trying to speak a language you've only read about but never heard spoken.

This unfamiliarity gets misread as unwillingness or resistance. Actually, it's absence. You're searching for something that was never installed. There's no neural pathway worn smooth by repeated experiences of being treated gently when you made mistakes, being comforted when you hurt, being told your needs mattered. The infrastructure isn't there.

Self-compassion is physiologically disorienting for trauma survivors. Your body knows tension, contraction, bracing. Those states feel familiar. Softness feels like stepping into a room with no floor.

Research shows self-compassion can be learned at any age. If you didn't learn it in childhood, you can learn it now. You're building pathways your system never had the chance to form.

This chapter covers why self-compassion feels physically uncomfortable, how to work with a nervous system that has no memory of gentleness, how to create new relational patterns with yourself, and how to train your body to tolerate feeling cared for.

Why Being Nice to Yourself Feels Impossible or Dangerous

Your body has an alarm system for self-kindness. The moment you try to be gentle with yourself, something activates. Your shoulders tense. Your jaw clenches. A voice says "This is stupid" or "You don't have time for this" or "Other people have real problems." Underneath the voice is a sensation: discomfort, wrongness, a feeling that you're doing something you shouldn't.

This is a somatic pattern, and it developed for reasons.

When you never received consistent gentleness as a child, your nervous system adapted to its absence. It learned to function without softness. Being hard on yourself became the baseline, the neutral state, the way things are. Self-criticism wasn't seen as a problem because nothing else was modeled. You didn't know you were supposed to feel differently.

Now, as an adult, when you attempt self-compassion, your body registers it as unfamiliar. Unfamiliar doesn't mean pleasant or exciting to a traumatized nervous system. Unfamiliar means potentially unsafe. The body prefers familiar pain over unknown comfort.

How Your Body Erases Discomfort Before You Notice It

Pay attention the next time you're struggling. What's your immediate internal response?

For most trauma survivors, the reflex is to minimize, dismiss, or override. You're exhausted, and you tell yourself you're fine. You're in pain, and you push through. You're sad, and you ignore it. Someone asks how you are, and you say "Good" automatically, even when you're falling apart.

This is a trained response. Your system learned early that acknowledging struggle led nowhere helpful, so it stopped acknowledging. The recognition that you're hurting, that you need something, that this is difficult... these observations never form. There's nothing to be compassionate toward because you've already erased the suffering from your awareness.

Self-compassion requires first noticing that you're in pain. If you can't register discomfort, you can't respond to it with care.

The Discomfort of Receiving

Some trauma survivors can be endlessly generous with others yet freeze when someone tries to give to them. A friend offers help, and your whole body says "No, I'm fine, I don't need anything." Someone compliments you, and you deflect immediately. You feel intensely uncomfortable receiving care, attention, or kindness from outside.

This same discomfort appears when you try to give yourself care. Your nervous system treats self-compassion like receiving from someone else. Receiving was never safe. Perhaps receiving in childhood meant owing something. Perhaps it meant being indebted, controlled, or obligated. Perhaps kindness always had strings attached. Your body remembers, even when your mind doesn't, that receiving care came at a cost.

Now when you try to be kind to yourself, your body tenses the same way. "What's the catch? What will this cost me? What am I setting myself up for?"

Your body isn't rejecting care because it's wrong. It has no template for what to do with it.

The Withdrawal of Familiar Pressure

You might notice that being hard on yourself feels like it gives you structure. The internal tightness that kept you moving creates a sense of forward momentum, even when it's exhausting. That tension feels like what's keeping you functional.

What happens when you remove it, even briefly? For many trauma survivors, the absence of that constant drive creates panic. Without it, you don't know what to do. You feel untethered, directionless, like you might float away or collapse entirely. Self-compassion removes the familiar tension, and the resulting spaciousness feels terrifying.

You've been functioning despite the tension. Your nervous system doesn't know that yet. It associates survival with tightness and believes softness equals danger.

The Physical Sensation of Being Wrong

This is the core issue: self-compassion feels wrong in your body. You're violating a long-standing rule your body still believes in. Your chest might feel tight. Your stomach might churn. You might feel exposed, embarrassed, or like you're getting away with something you shouldn't.

These sensations are your nervous system's learned response. In childhood, being gentle with yourself (resting when tired, crying when hurt, asking for help) may have been met with punishment, mockery, or neglect. Your body learned: self-gentleness leads to bad outcomes. Now it tries to protect you from those outcomes by making self-gentleness feel bad.

The sensation of wrongness is actually your body trying to keep you safe using outdated information. It's evidence that your body needs new information.

When Needs Disappear

Many trauma survivors describe not feeling their needs until they've escalated to crisis. You don't notice you're hungry until you're shaking. You don't notice you're tired until you can't think straight. You don't notice you're overwhelmed until you're having a breakdown.

This happens because the early signals (the gentle indicators that you need something) were trained out of you. As a child, expressing small needs ("I'm a little hungry," "I'm getting tired," "This is hard for me") was ignored, punished, or made you feel burdensome. So you learned to ignore those signals until they became so loud you couldn't.

Self-compassion requires catching needs when they're still small. If you can't feel them at that stage, you can't respond to them compassionately. You only respond in crisis mode, which feels like damage control.

EXERCISE: Noticing Self-Kindness Resistance

This week, pay attention to moments when you automatically deny, minimize, or override your own experience.

Daily tracking: Each day, notice 2-3 moments when you:

Moment 1:

What I was experiencing: ____

My automatic response: ____

What I felt in my body when I denied/minimized: ______________________________

Moment 2:

What I was experiencing: ____

My automatic response: ____

What I felt in my body when I denied/minimized: ______________________________

Moment 3:

What I was experiencing: ____

My automatic response: ____

What I felt in my body when I denied/minimized: ______________________________

End of week reflection: What pattern do you notice? When are you most likely to erase your own struggle?

____

____

Experiment: Choose one small moment of discomfort this week. Instead of your automatic response, try simply acknowledging it: "This is hard right now." Notice what happens in your body when you don't deny the difficulty.

____

____

The Three Pillars of Self-Compassion for Trauma Survivors

Self-compassion has three components that work together. Understanding them makes the practice less abstract and more concrete.

Pillar 1: Self-Kindness

Self-kindness means responding to your pain without adding punishment to it.

When you're struggling, notice your immediate response. For most trauma survivors, the default is to escalate suffering. When you're in pain, you attack yourself for being in pain. When you make a mistake, you make yourself feel worse about making the mistake. You learned to be your own worst enemy.

Try this instead: Imagine a small, frightened animal. It's hurt and scared. Would you kick it for being hurt? Would you tell it it's pathetic? No. You'd speak softly. You'd move slowly. You'd try to make it feel safe.

It doesn't need fixing. It needs gentleness.

Your frightened, hurting self is that animal. Self-kindness is talking to yourself the way you'd talk to something vulnerable that needs care.

An injured animal still needs to heal, might need boundaries, might need behavior change. Healing happens faster in an environment of care than an environment of attack.

Practice it somatically: When you notice you're suffering, place your hand on your chest or your own shoulder. Physical touch activates the parasympathetic nervous system (the part that signals safety). You don't have to believe anything. Just put your hand somewhere comforting and keep it there while you're in pain.

Pillar 2: Common Humanity

Common humanity means recognizing that suffering connects you to others.

Trauma taught you the opposite. Your pain made you different, isolated, wrong. You learned to hide your struggles because revealing them meant being alone with them. Now when you suffer, you instinctively pull away from others, certain that your pain makes you unlovable or incomprehensible.

Common humanity shifts this: You're struggling right now, and so are many others. Your specific circumstances are yours, yet the experience of struggle is universal. You're human.

This is about recognizing that needing help, feeling overwhelmed, making mistakes, and being in pain are part of being alive. They don't make you defective.

When you catch yourself thinking "I'm the only one who can't handle this" or "Everyone else has it together," notice that you're isolating yourself in your pain. Then deliberately think: "Other people are struggling today too. I'm not alone in finding life hard sometimes."

Practice it physically: When you feel isolated in your suffering, imagine standing in a room full of people who are also struggling today. You're ordinary in your suffering. This is what humans do: we hurt, we struggle, we need care. Feel yourself as part of that room, not outside it.

Pillar 3: Mindfulness

Mindfulness in self-compassion means staying present with pain without making it bigger or smaller than it is.

Trauma often pulls you out of the present. Either by shutting down sensations or overwhelming you with them. Erasure means refusing to acknowledge what's real. Catastrophizing means projecting into a terrible future.

Mindfulness is simpler: "Right now, in this moment, I'm in pain. It hurts. And I'm here with it."

You're not saying "This will never end" (future).

You're not saying "I shouldn't feel this way" (judgment).

You're not saying "It's not that bad" (denial).

Just: "This hurts. I'm feeling it. I can be with this."

Practice it in your body: When you're overwhelmed, don't try to think your way to calm. Instead, feel your feet on the ground. Notice five things you can see. Feel the air moving in and out of your lungs. These physical anchors keep you present with what's actually happening instead of spiraling into what you fear will happen or denying what's real.

How They Work Together

You need all three pillars. One or two won't hold the structure.

Kindness without common humanity: "I'm being nice to myself, yet I'm still uniquely damaged."

Common humanity without kindness: "Everyone suffers, so what? I still feel terrible."

Mindfulness without the other two: "I'm aware I'm suffering" (cold, no warmth).

Together: "I'm in pain right now [mindfulness]. This is part of being human. Others are hurting too [common humanity]. I deserve gentleness in this moment [self-kindness]."

When you're suffering, place your hand on your chest, feel your feet on the ground, and say (out loud or internally):

"This is really hard right now. I'm not alone in struggling. I'm allowed to be kind to myself while I work through this."

Your nervous system won't believe these words immediately. You're not trying to believe. You're trying to practice. The neural pathways form through repetition.

EXERCISE: Three Pillars Practice

Choose a current struggle (something manageable, not your deepest trauma):

____

Apply each pillar with your body, not just your mind:

Self-Kindness - Physical Action:

Place both hands over your heart. Feel the warmth. While your hands are there, say: "*This is painful, and I'm allowed to comfort myself.*"

What did you notice in your body?

____

____

Common Humanity - Visualization:

Close your eyes. Imagine yourself in a room filled with people who are also struggling today. You're not separate from them. You're standing among them. Everyone here is hurting in some way.

What shifted when you imagined this?

____

____

Mindfulness - Sensory Anchoring:

Don't analyze your struggle. Instead, name three physical sensations you're feeling right now:

1. ____
2. ____
3. ____

Complete Response:

Put your hand on your chest again and say: "*I'm struggling with __________________________ right now. This is hard, and I'm not the only person who finds this hard. I can be gentle with myself while this is difficult.*"

Daily practice: Do this once per day this week with whatever struggle appears.

Reparenting the Child Who Never Felt Safe

Reparenting is about developing a capacity you never had the chance to learn: the ability to be a reliable source of safety for yourself.

Most people learn how to self-soothe, self-comfort, and self-reassure by internalizing how their caregivers did those things for them. If your caregivers didn't provide consistent comfort, you never internalized the process. You developed adult responsibilities without ever developing the internal capacity for comfort. The skill was never taught.

Reparenting is teaching yourself now what you should have learned then.

Recognizing When the Younger Part Appears

You're not always operating from your adult self. Sometimes, without realizing it, you slip into a younger state. You feel small. You feel powerless. You feel the way you felt at eight, or twelve, or fifteen.

This happens when you're triggered, overwhelmed, or in situations that echo childhood dynamics. The adult part of you goes offline, and a younger part takes over (the part that learned the original survival strategies).

When this happens, you need a different approach. The younger part doesn't respond to logic or adult reasoning. It needs what children need: to feel safe, to be seen, to know someone's paying attention.

Start noticing when you feel young. Your body will tell you: you might feel very small physically, or helpless, or desperately want someone to tell you what to do. When you notice this, instead of judging yourself for "being immature," try: "A younger part of me is here right now. What does this part need?"

Building Trust with Yourself Over Time

The younger part of you has evidence that you can't be trusted. You've overridden your limits for years, ignored pain, criticized relentlessly, made promises and broken them. Why should that young part believe you'll take care of them now?

You can't tell them once "I'll take care of you" and expect immediate trust. Trust builds through consistent, repeated actions over time.

This means: When you say you'll rest, actually rest. When you notice you're overwhelmed, actually take a break. When you promise yourself something, follow through. Each time you do what you said you'd do, you're giving the younger part evidence that you're reliable.

Apologies are words. Trust is built through action.

Developing New Proof of Safety

The younger part of you has a catalog of evidence that the world isn't safe and that you can't trust others to take care of you. You can't erase that evidence. You can start building a new catalog: evidence that things are different now.

This happens in small moments:

- You're scared, and instead of pushing through, you pause and assess whether there's actual danger.
- You make a mistake, and instead of the catastrophe you expect, you handle it calmly.
- You set a boundary, and instead of abandonment, the relationship continues.
- You rest when you're tired, and instead of everything falling apart, things are fine.

Each small piece of evidence updates the internal model. "Maybe it's safe to have needs now. Maybe I can stop performing perfectly and still be okay. Maybe I don't have to be hypervigilant every moment."

You're showing them through lived experience that their old predictions don't match current reality.

The Practice of Gentle Consistency

Healing isn't dramatic. It's quiet, repetitive, and often boring. It's doing the same small caring actions day after day until they become automatic.

Create tiny, repeatable rituals that signal care:

- Each morning, before checking your phone, take three slow breaths and say "Good morning" to yourself.
- When you get home, spend two quiet minutes of breathing before launching into tasks.
- Before bed, place your hand on your chest and say "You made it through today."

These are small, consistent contacts with yourself that say: "I'm paying attention to you. You matter. I'm here."

Over weeks and months, these micro-moments accumulate. Your nervous system learns: "Oh. This is what it feels like to be cared for regularly. This is what 'home' feels like."

Letting the Younger Part Have Preferences

Part of reparenting is letting the younger part influence your life in small ways. What did you love before trauma narrowed your world? What brought you joy before you learned joy was frivolous?

Give that part permission to want things:

- If they loved drawing, buy crayons and a coloring book.
- If they loved being outside, take ten minutes to stand in the sun.
- If they found comfort in a specific food, eat it without guilt.
- If they loved a certain movie, watch it even though it's "childish."

You're acknowledging that part of you was forced to grow up too fast and lost access to things that felt good. You're giving them back a little bit of what was taken.

EXERCISE: Building Internal Trust

Part 1 - Identify When You Feel Young:

This week, notice moments when you feel smaller, younger, or more helpless than your actual age. Before writing, notice how your body feels when the younger part appears. Describe one moment:

What was happening: ____

How old did you feel:____

What did that younger part need: ____________________________________

Part 2 - Make One Small Promise:

Choose one small, concrete action you can do this week to care for yourself. Make it specific and achievable.

I promise myself I will: ____

(Examples: "I will go to bed by 10pm three nights this week," "I will take a 10-minute walk outside twice," "I will eat breakfast sitting down, not standing")

Part 3 - Track Your Follow-Through:

Each day you keep your promise, mark it:

Day 1: ☐ Day 2: ☐ Day 3: ☐ Day 4: ☐ Day 5: ☐ Day 6: ☐ Day 7: ☐

Part 4 - Build the Evidence:

At the end of the week, if you kept your promise, write:

"I said I would ____, and I did.

This is evidence that I'm reliable. I'm learning to trust myself."

If you didn't keep your promise, write:

"I wasn't able to follow through. What got in the way? What would make this promise more realistic?"

____

____

Next Week: Make the same promise or adjust it to be more realistic. Keep building the evidence.

Self-Care as Resistance Against Old Survival Patterns

Your body isn't used to receiving care. Your nervous system adapted to functioning in a chronically depleted state. It learned to run without consistent nourishment, rest, or gentleness.

Now when you try to introduce regular care, your body doesn't know what to do with it. It's like reintroducing warmth to a body that's been cold for too long. You have to do it slowly, carefully, or the system rejects it.

Self-care for trauma survivors is about retraining a nervous system to tolerate feeling good.

The Body's Intolerance for Positive States

Notice what happens when something good occurs. You get a compliment, and you immediately deflect. You have a nice moment, and you brace for it to end. You start to relax, and anxiety spikes.

Your nervous system has been trained to expect threat, pain, and instability. When things feel good, your body interprets it as the calm before the storm. "This won't last. Better stay alert. Don't let your guard down."

This is a survival mechanism. Your body learned that moments of ease were temporary and often preceded something bad. So it refuses to settle into feeling good. Staying tense is safer.

Your body prepares for impact even when there's nothing coming.

Retraining this pattern means deliberately creating small experiences of ease and staying present for them instead of bracing for disaster. You're teaching your body: "Sometimes good things happen and nothing bad follows. It's safe to feel okay."

Micro-Doses of Care

You can't go from total self-neglect to perfect self-care overnight. Your nervous system will reject the change as too foreign, too unsafe.

Start with doses so small they don't trigger resistance:

- Drink one full glass of water slowly, paying attention to the sensation.
- Stand in sunlight for sixty seconds and notice the warmth on your skin.
- Stretch for two minutes and feel your muscles release.
- Take three deep breaths before getting out of bed.

You're introducing care in amounts small enough that your nervous system doesn't panic and shut down.

Over time, as your body learns that care doesn't lead to catastrophe, you can increase the dose. If you start too big ("I'm going to meditate for an hour and meal prep for the week"), your system will reject it, you'll fail, and you'll have more evidence that you can't care for yourself.

Habituation to Safety

Your body needs repetition to learn that care is safe. One good meal doesn't teach your body it will be fed regularly. One night of rest doesn't teach your body it's allowed to relax. One kind word to yourself doesn't rewire decades of self-attack.

The same small act, repeated daily for weeks, starts to create a new baseline. Your body begins to expect care instead of brace against its absence.

This is habituation: exposure to a stimulus over time until it no longer triggers a stress response. You're habituating your nervous system to kindness.

Create one non-negotiable daily ritual (something so small it feels almost pointless):

- Every morning, before anything else, drink water.
- Every evening, before bed, wash your face slowly.
- Every time you eat, take the first three bites without distraction.

The ritual itself matters less than the consistency. You're training your body: "Every day, at this time, something caring happens. You can count on this."

After weeks of consistency, your body starts to recognize the pattern. The internal resistance decreases. Care starts to feel less foreign.

The Discomfort of Receiving Care

When you do something caring for yourself, notice the discomfort that arises. Maybe you feel guilty. Maybe you feel silly. Maybe you feel like you're wasting time or being selfish.

These feelings are your nervous system's way of saying "This is unfamiliar, therefore potentially unsafe." It's trying to get you to stop and return to the familiar (harsh) baseline.

Don't try to argue with the discomfort or make it go away. Just name it: "There's the discomfort. My body isn't used to this yet. That's okay. I'm going to keep doing it anyway."

The discomfort will decrease over time, only if you continue the practice despite the discomfort. If you stop every time it feels wrong, you never give your nervous system the chance to learn that it's actually safe.

Building Tolerance for Feeling Good

This is the ultimate goal: increasing your nervous system's capacity to tolerate moments of ease without immediately expecting disaster.

Start noticing when you feel okay (not ecstatic, just okay) and practice staying there for an extra moment instead of immediately looking for what's wrong or what you should be doing.

You feel content after a meal. Instead of rushing to the next task, stay in the feeling for ten seconds. "I feel satisfied right now. This is what okay feels like."

You finish something and feel briefly accomplished. Instead of immediately thinking of the next thing, pause. "I did this. It feels good to complete something."

These small extensions of ease (staying present for feeling okay instead of immediately moving past it) slowly expand your window of tolerance for wellbeing.

EXERCISE: Building Your Care Routine

Part 1 - Choose Your One Non-Negotiable Ritual:

Select one tiny, specific action you'll do every day this week at the same time. It should take less than 5 minutes.

My ritual: ____

Time of day: ____

(Examples: "Drink water while still in bed," "Take 3 deep breaths before lunch," "Spend 2 minutes stretching before bed")

Part 2 - Track Your Discomfort:

Each day after your ritual, rate your discomfort level (0-10):

Day 1: ___ Day 2: ___ Day 3: ___ Day 4: ___ Day 5: ___ Day 6: ___ Day 7: ___

Part 3 - Notice the Sensations:

When discomfort or resistance appears, describe the physical sensation:

____

____

Don't try to change it. Just notice it and continue the ritual anyway.

Part 4 - What Your Body is Learning:

At the end of the week, complete this:

"I did ____ every day for 7 days.

My body is learning that:

____

____

Chapter 10:
Relationships When Your Attachment System Is Wounded

"We're never so vulnerable than when we trust someone—but paradoxically, if we cannot trust, neither can we find love or joy." — Walter Anderson

You're sitting across from someone who says they care about you. Your chest tightens. Your mind races through escape routes. You want to believe them, but every cell in your body screams that closeness equals danger. So you smile and change the subject, or pick a fight about nothing, or suddenly remember you need to leave. Later, alone, you ache for exactly what you just ran from.

When the people meant to protect you were the ones who hurt you, your attachment system learns an impossible equation: the thing required for safety is itself the source of danger. These patterns aren't character flaws—they're strategies born from environments where connection came with threat.

You might test people relentlessly, creating small crises to see if they'll stay. Or you flee the moment relationships become stable because your nervous system treats security as suspicious. The specific patterns vary, but the underlying bind stays the same: you need connection to heal, yet connection activates every defense you have.

This chapter shows you how childhood experiences create specific relationship patterns, how to recognize which patterns you carry, how to build trust incrementally, and how to express needs without triggering collapse in yourself or others. The work requires doing things that feel unnatural—staying when you want to run, speaking when you want to hide, trusting in small doses when your instinct screams to trust no one.

These patterns can change. With awareness and practice, secure connection becomes possible even when attachment trauma shaped your earliest experiences.

How Childhood Trauma Creates Adult Relationship Chaos

Attachment theory starts with a simple premise: humans develop expectations about relationships based on how caregivers respond to them in early childhood. When caregivers are consistently available, attuned, and safe, children develop secure attachment. When caregivers are neglectful, inconsistent, abusive, or emotionally unavailable, children develop insecure patterns that persist into adulthood.

The specific childhood experiences that wound attachment systems show up in predictable ways in adult relationships.

Neglect in childhood often reappears like this: In romantic relationships, you apologize for sending more than one text message. You disappear for days when struggling because asking for support feels like imposing. When your partner asks "What's wrong?" you say "Nothing" even when you're falling apart. At work, you never mention when you're overwhelmed until you're at the breaking point. With friends, you show up for them constantly but can't imagine calling when you need something.

Inconsistency in childhood creates this pattern: You're hypervigilant to shifts in your partner's mood or attention. They respond to your text an hour later than usual and you're convinced they're pulling away. They seem slightly distant one evening and you spiral into panic. You can never fully relax into connection because you're always scanning for the moment things will shift. Even when your partner is being warm, you're preparing for when they won't be. You interpret neutral behavior as rejection because you learned that warmth could turn to coldness without warning.

Abuse in childhood shows up as: You choose partners who are volatile or cruel because calm, kind people feel alien. When someone treats you consistently well, you keep waiting for the harm you're sure is coming. Or you misread healthy boundaries as rejection and minor frustrations as rage. During sex, you freeze or dissociate even with safe partners because intimacy learned to pair with threat. You might pick fights when things feel too good, unconsciously recreating the chaos that your body recognizes as normal.

Emotional unavailability in childhood manifests as: You're drawn to partners who are distracted, shut down, or can't access their feelings. You feel profound loneliness even in long-term relationships. When you try to talk about emotions, you hit a wall—they change the subject, minimize, or go blank. You've learned to accept emotional isolation as the price of companionship. Or you become the emotionally unavailable one, maintaining surface-level relationships while keeping your inner world hidden.

Enmeshment in childhood creates: Panic when partners want closeness because it feels like being swallowed. You can't tell where you end and your partner begins—you absorb their moods, adopt their opinions, lose track of what you actually want. After time together, you feel depleted or erased. Or you swing the other way: rigid independence, refusal to merge with anyone, a terror of depending on others because dependence once meant losing yourself entirely.

These experiences don't just create vague "trust issues." They create specific relational rules you follow without knowing you're following them. Rules like: *If they're not anxious about me, they don't actually care. If I don't have to chase them, it's not real love. If they see who I really am, they'll leave. If I show need, I become a burden they'll eventually resent.*

These rules operate beneath conscious awareness, determining who you choose, how you behave, and what you expect. When someone breaks the rules—responds when you expect distance, stays when you expect abandonment, accepts you when you expect rejection—it doesn't feel like relief. It feels wrong, suspicious, or simply invisible because your system isn't looking for that kind of response.

The reenactment compulsion adds another layer. You unconsciously seek out people who resemble the parent who hurt you and work to get from them what you never got in childhood. You choose the emotionally distant partner and exhaust yourself trying to make them open up. You date the critical person and contort yourself trying to earn their approval. The familiar feels like fate, like "the one," even when the familiar means repeating harm.

You're not trying to hurt yourself. Some part of you believes that if you can make *this* relationship work, it will retroactively heal the original wound. It won't—you can't resolve childhood attachment trauma through adult relationships with people who recreate the original dynamic—but the drive to try runs deep.

Here's what makes this particularly difficult: when healthy relationships arrive, they often feel wrong. If your nervous system learned that love includes anxiety and proving yourself, someone who is secure and consistently kind won't register as romantic. They'll register as boring. You might create drama to generate the adrenaline you associate with passion. You might leave good people to return to chaos because chaos is what your body knows as connection.

Certain situations trigger your trauma responses even in safe relationships. Your partner doesn't text back for three hours and abandonment terror floods you. They seem irritated and shame crashes down. They want to spend the weekend together and you feel trapped. They need emotional support and you panic that you'll fail them. The intensity isn't about the current situation—it's about old wounds activated by present circumstances. You're responding to the past while your partner stands confused in the present, unsure what they did to cause this reaction.

The cycle that maintains relationship difficulties: attachment wound from childhood creates anxious, avoidant, or chaotic patterns in adult relationships. These patterns prevent secure connection. The absence of secure connection confirms the wound: *See? People aren't safe. I'm not lovable.* The pattern continues.

Breaking the cycle requires seeing it first. Once you recognize what you're doing and why, you can practice different responses even when they feel unnatural. The new behaviors won't feel right initially—they'll feel vulnerable or just wrong—but with repetition, your nervous system can learn that connection doesn't always lead to harm.

✎ EXERCISE: Mapping Your Relationship Timeline

This exercise maps how childhood dynamics show up across your adult relationships.

Choose 3-4 significant relationships (romantic, close friendships, or work relationships where attachment patterns showed up)

For each relationship, complete the table:

Relationship	My Role (What did I do?)	My Core Fear	Their Pattern

Examples for "My Role": chaser, distancer, caretaker, accommodator, crisis creator

Examples for "Core Fear": abandonment, engulfment, being too much, being inadequate

Examples for "Their Pattern": unavailable, critical, smothering, unpredictable

Connection to Childhood:

Which childhood dynamic do you see repeated across these relationships?

____

____

____

Pattern Recognition:

What role do you play most often? ____

What fear shows up repeatedly? ____

What type of person do you tend to choose? _____________________________________

Recognizing Your Attachment Style and Trauma Responses

Attachment styles are strategies you developed to navigate your early environment. Understanding yours gives you a map of what patterns to interrupt.

Anxious/Preoccupied Attachment makes relationships feel like life or death. You're terrified of abandonment. Your emotional state depends on how others treat you—when they're close, you're okay; when distant, you're in crisis. In relationships, you pursue closeness intensely, need frequent contact, interpret small distance as rejection, and struggle being alone. When someone pulls away, you protest through repeated contact or creating situations that demand their attention because any distance feels catastrophic. Your core fear: abandonment.

Avoidant/Dismissive Attachment makes closeness feel threatening. You value independence intensely and don't like needing others. In relationships, you maintain distance, avoid commitment, shut down emotionally during conflict, and feel suffocated by others' needs. You minimize your own needs or deny having them. When stress arises, you cope by distancing—becoming cold, going silent, or leaving. Your core fear: engulfment.

Disorganized/Fearful-Avoidant Attachment creates simultaneous craving and terror of closeness. You're both anxious and avoidant. In relationships, you swing between pursuing and distancing, sometimes within the same conversation. You chase someone until they reciprocate, then panic and push them away. You want intimacy but sabotage it when it arrives. You test people excessively or oscillate between idealizing and devaluing partners. Your core fears: both abandonment and engulfment simultaneously.

These styles can vary by relationship type. You might be anxious romantically but avoidant with friends.

How Styles Interact: Two anxious people escalate each other's fear. Two avoidant people maintain stable distance. Anxious-avoidant pairings create pursue-withdraw cycles where one chases and the other distances, each intensifying the other's pattern.

Beyond attachment styles, your trauma responses appear in relationship-specific ways:

Anxious + Fight looks like: sending multiple texts demanding response, creating conflict to force engagement, getting angry when they need space

Anxious + Fawn looks like: losing all boundaries to keep them close, saying yes to everything, accommodating to the point of self-erasure

Avoidant + Flight looks like: ghosting mid-conversation, ending relationships abruptly, physically leaving during conflict

Avoidant + Freeze looks like: going silent during important conversations, shutting down emotionally when they want closeness, dissociating during intimacy

Disorganized + Oscillation looks like: attacking then apologizing desperately, demanding closeness then rejecting it, swinging between all four responses chaotically

Understanding both your attachment style and dominant trauma response shows you what's happening when relationships trigger you. You're having predictable responses based on your history, not being "impossible to love."

✏ EXERCISE: Attachment Style and Conflict Mapping

Part 1: Identify Your Style

In romantic relationships, I'm primarily: ☐ Anxious ☐ Avoidant ☐ Disorganized ☐ Secure

My core fear is: ☐ Abandonment ☐ Engulfment ☐ Both ☐ Neither strongly

Part 2: Your Trauma Response Pattern

When relationship stress happens, I typically: ☐ Fight ☐ Flight ☐ Freeze ☐ Fawn

Part 3: Conflict Scene

Describe a typical conflict moment with a partner or close friend:

What triggered the conflict?

____

What did you do? (specific actions, words, body language)

____

What did the other person do?

____

Which attachment style was operating in you? ____

Which trauma response were you using? ____

Part 4: Pattern Recognition

This same pattern (your action + their reaction) has happened in _____ other relationships

What would a different response look like?

____

____

Building Trust When Everyone Feels Like a Threat

You need relationships to heal attachment trauma, but attachment trauma makes relationships feel dangerous. You can't heal in isolation, but connection activates your defenses.

Trust isn't all-or-nothing. Like other practices in this workbook, you work in small doses. You share small vulnerabilities and observe responses. If someone responds with care consistently, you share something slightly bigger.

Start with relationships where stakes are lower. Don't practice with your most important or triggering people. Start with a therapist, support group member, acquaintance, or online community. Build the pathways in safer contexts first.

Learn what trustworthy behavior looks like in daily life. Your hypervigilance scans for danger constantly, but you might not recognize safety:

- They text when they say they'll text
- When you say "I don't want to talk about this now," they don't keep pushing in messages
- When they mess up, they don't say "You're too sensitive"
- They show up on time or give advance notice if plans change
- They don't share what you told them privately with their friends
- When you set a boundary, they don't punish you with silence or coldness

Notice these micro-indicators. Your nervous system might dismiss them ("This is temporary," "They're pretending"), but consciously track trustworthy behavior when it happens.

Test trust through relationship-specific vulnerabilities:

Share that you're having a hard week. Do they respond with care or change the subject?

Express a preference that differs from theirs. Do they respect it or pressure you to agree?

Set a small boundary around plans or timing. Do they honor it or guilt-trip you?

Share a feeling about something they did. Do they listen or get defensive?

Mention something from your past. Do they hold it with care or use it against you later?

Ask for what you need. Do they try to accommodate or make you feel demanding?

If their response feels unsafe at any point, you pause or step back. You're gathering data about whether this person is trustworthy, not forcing trust because you "should."

Reality-check your responses. When you feel suspicious or afraid, ask: What is this person actually doing right now? What concrete evidence do I have in this moment? What would someone neutral say about this situation?

Sometimes your caution is warranted—your intuition picks up real red flags. Sometimes you're responding to the past. Distinguishing takes practice and often requires outside perspective.

Repair after self-sabotage differently based on your style:

Anxious: "I sent fifteen texts last night. That was my panic talking, not your worth or our relationship."

Avoidant: "I disappeared for three days. That wasn't about you doing anything wrong—I shut down when closeness scares me."

Disorganized: "I asked you to come over, then told you to leave an hour later. That's my pattern of wanting and fearing closeness simultaneously. I'm working on it."

This kind of repair teaches your nervous system that relationships can survive your patterns and mistakes. When trust gets broken—and sometimes it will—distinguish between minor breaches with repair versus patterns without repair. Someone forgets something important but acknowledges it and makes amends: watch how they repair, not just that they failed. Someone repeatedly hurts you and either doesn't acknowledge it or acknowledges but doesn't change behavior: that's information about safety.

Not every breach means the relationship ends, but patterns of unrepaired harm mean this person isn't trustworthy right now. Trust broken doesn't prove you were right never to trust anyone. It means this particular person wasn't trustworthy, and you gained information.

EXERCISE: Trust-Building with Prediction Check

This exercise addresses the gap between what you expect to happen and what actually happens when you take relational risks.

Step 1: Choose a Low-Stakes Person

Someone relatively safe where stakes aren't too high:

Person/context: ____

Step 2: Identify One Small Vulnerability

What will you share? (opinion, need, boundary, feeling)

____

Step 3: Prediction

Before you share, what do you predict will happen?

____

____

How certain are you this will happen? (circle one)

Completely certain Very likely Somewhat likely Unsure

Step 4: Share and Record Reality

What actually happened when you shared:

____

____

Did they show trustworthy behaviors? ☐ Yes ☐ Somewhat ☐ No

Step 5: Compare Prediction to Reality

Prediction: ____

Reality: ____

Were they different? ☐ Yes ☐ No

If yes, what does this tell you about your expectations?

____

____

Step 6: Next Step

Based on their actual response (not your prediction):

Next thing to share: ____

Or, if unsafe: What did you learn about this person?

____

____

Communicating Needs Without Triggering Fight-or-Flight

In childhood, expressing needs led to rejection or punishment. Conflict meant danger. Your nervous system learned that speaking up threatens survival.

Now, as an adult, even small requests trigger your trauma response before your thinking brain can assess whether the situation is actually dangerous.

Basic communication tools, adapted by attachment style:

Use "I" statements: "I feel unheard when I'm talking and there's no acknowledgment. I need a signal that you're listening."

Be specific: "When I'm stressed, it helps when you ask how I'm doing and just listen without trying to fix it."

Validate their perspective: "I know you're busy and didn't mean to forget. I still felt hurt that our plans got canceled without notice."

Request, don't demand: "Would you be willing to give me a heads-up if you need to cancel plans?"

But here's where attachment style matters:

Anxious attachment communicates like this when triggered: Over-explains everything, sends paragraph-long texts, asks for reassurance repeatedly, apologizes for having needs, frames every request as "I don't want to be demanding, but..." You're so afraid of being "too much" that you bury the actual need in qualifiers and apologies.

What to practice: State the need once, clearly, without the apologetic preamble. "I need more check-ins during the week" instead of "I know you're busy and I don't want to be annoying, but if it's not too much trouble, maybe we could..."

Avoidant attachment communicates like this when triggered: Minimizes problems, says "It's fine" when it's not, changes the subject when emotions come up, gives one-word responses, physically or emotionally exits conversations. You protect yourself by shutting down communication entirely.

What to practice: Name one feeling before you minimize it. "I'm frustrated about this" before saying "but it doesn't matter." Stay in the conversation for two more minutes than feels comfortable instead of leaving immediately.

Disorganized attachment communicates like this when triggered: Starts soft, then escalates into anger or desperation. Or opens with a need but retreats into silence before the conversation finishes. Or swings between "I need you" and "Leave me alone" in the same exchange. You want connection but panic mid-conversation.

What to practice: Notice when you're about to swing. Pause and name it: "I'm getting activated and might push you away in a minute. I want to stay in this conversation, but I need to slow down."

Regulate before difficult conversations. If you're outside your window of tolerance, communication will fail. Check your state. If you're not regulated enough, postpone: "I want to talk about this, but I need an hour to settle first." If you become dysregulated during the conversation, explicitly pause instead of either continuing to fight or disappearing: "I need five minutes. I'm getting triggered and I want to finish this conversation, but not like this."

Navigate conflict differently based on your pattern:

When it escalates, pause: "This is getting too intense. Let's take twenty minutes and come back." Then actually return at the agreed time.

Look for competing needs underneath: Partner A needs alone time after work. Partner B needs connection. Both are legitimate. The solution addresses both: "Can I have thirty minutes alone when I get home, then we spend time together after?"

Repair immediately: "I'm sorry, that came out wrong. Let me try again" or "I'm being defensive. What I meant was..."

When communication isn't safe: If someone exploits your attachment needs to control you—threatens abandonment to make you comply, uses your fear of being "too much" to shut down your needs, punishes you with withdrawal for having feelings—the problem isn't your communication skills. It's that the relationship isn't safe. Signs include: they punish you for having needs, they gaslight you, they escalate to threats or aggression, they turn every conversation into your failures.

If this is happening, the work is deciding whether the relationship can continue and what protection you need, not practicing better "I" statements.

EXERCISE: Need Communication with Attachment Awareness

Step 1: Identify One Need

What's one need you have in a current relationship that you haven't expressed?

____

Step 2: Attachment Fear Check

What's your attachment fear connected to this need?

☐ If I express this, they'll leave (abandonment)

☐ If I express this, they'll control me or I'll lose myself (engulfment)

☐ Both fears are present (disorganized)

Step 3: Write It Using Formula

I feel ____

When____

I need ____

Would you be willing to ____?

Step 4: Regulate and Communicate

Before the conversation:

Am I regulated enough? ☐ Yes ☐ No (need to ground first)

After the conversation:

Their response: ____

My attachment fear: ☐ Was confirmed ☐ Was challenged ☐ Partially both

Step 5: What My Attachment System Learned

What did this experience teach your attachment system?

☐ Expressing needs led to rejection (confirms old pattern)

☐ Expressing needs was received okay (challenges old pattern)

☐ Mixed—need was heard but fear was still present

This specific evidence from today:

____

____

____

Next practice:

What's one other small need you could express this week?

____

Chapter 11: Boundaries You Never Learned to Build

"The only people who get upset about you setting boundaries are the ones who were benefiting from you having none." — Unknown

Picture a house with no doors. Rooms that blend into one another, spaces where anyone can enter at will, no way to close off what's yours. You can't rest because there's nowhere private. You can't protect your belongings because there's no distinction between what's yours and what's shared. You exist in a state of ongoing availability, unfiltered exposure.

This is what it means to live without boundaries.

You might notice it first as a physical sensation—a tightness in your throat when your phone rings, knowing you'll say yes even though you want to say no. A heaviness in your chest when someone asks for something you don't have the capacity to give. A sense of being occupied, colonized by other people's needs and expectations, with no territory that's truly your own.

Boundaries mark where your responsibility ends and someone else's begins. They define what you're willing to give, what you need to protect, how you want to be treated. For people raised in functional families, these lines form naturally. Adults demonstrate them through their own behavior: they decline invitations when tired, they ask before borrowing things, they respect closed doors and private conversations.

For people with C-PTSD, those reference points never existed. Your childhood home had no doors—metaphorically and sometimes literally. Adults entered your room without knocking. They read your diary, opened your mail, demanded access to your thoughts and feelings. They treated your body as communal property, your time as their resource, your emotional capacity as their right. When you tried to create separation, you were punished. When you said no, you faced consequences.

The lesson embedded itself deep: having limits invites danger.

Now you operate from one of two positions, or swing wildly between them. Either you've built fortress walls so thick that genuine connection can't penetrate—a defensive structure that keeps everyone at arm's length because letting anyone close means losing control. Or you exist with no separation at all, carrying everyone's problems and demands, unable to distinguish between what's yours to carry and what isn't.

Neither extreme creates actual safety. Fortress walls prevent intimacy. Complete porousness leads to depletion.

The cost shows up in your relationships, which become transactional—you give until resentment builds, then withdraw completely. It shows up in your body, which carries the exhaustion of constant over-giving. It shows up in your sense of self, which gets lost in the constant adjustment to what others need.

This chapter addresses a skill you were supposed to learn in childhood but didn't: how to mark your limits. You'll learn to recognize when your boundaries are being crossed, understand why protecting them feels life-threatening, and practice the physical and verbal actions that reinforce them. This isn't about becoming rigid or selfish. It's about creating structure—the kind that makes relationships sustainable and your life livable.

You need boundaries not to keep people out, but to know where you stand.

Why Saying No Feels Like Inviting Abandonment

Your body reacts to boundary-setting the way it would react to stepping off a cliff. Heart rate spikes. Breath shortens. The word "no" gets stuck somewhere between your brain and your mouth. This isn't a thought pattern—it's your body reenacting an old relational rule.

When you were young, separation wasn't safe. Attempts to create distance—saying you needed space, closing your bedroom door, refusing to share something private—triggered retaliation. Not always dramatic. Sometimes just a look, a tone shift, the sudden withdrawal of warmth. Your system registered the pattern: assertion leads to isolation. Having needs leads to expulsion.

The mechanism was straightforward. You said no to physical affection you didn't want, and the adult responded with hours of cold silence. You tried to keep a possession to yourself, and you were told you were selfish, ungenerous, bad. You expressed that something hurt you, and you were informed you were too sensitive, that you were making problems where none existed. You attempted to create privacy, and your door was removed from its hinges.

These weren't isolated incidents. They formed the architecture of your relational world. The message imprinted itself at a level below conscious thought: boundaries equal rejection.

Now, decades later, the same circuitry fires when you contemplate setting a limit. Your nervous system doesn't distinguish between then and now. It only knows: last time you did this, you were alone. Last time you protected yourself, you lost connection. The fear isn't irrational—it's rooted in past evidence.

Several forces drive the terror.

Fear of expulsion from the relationship. Not just being alone, but being cast out, marked as too difficult, too demanding, too much. The primitive part of your brain that formed in childhood still believes: if I require anything, I'll be discarded. Better to require nothing and stay included than to have needs and face exile.

Fear of retaliatory withdrawal. You've seen what happens when someone gets angry with you for setting limits. They don't just disagree—they disappear. Days of silence, sudden coldness, emotional punishment designed to make you regret ever trying to protect yourself. Your system learned: peace depends on total accommodation.

Fear of discovering you don't matter enough to be worth respecting. If you state a boundary and it's immediately violated, you're forced to confront something unbearable: your limits don't carry weight. You don't matter enough for someone to adjust their behavior. Setting boundaries risks exposing this hierarchical truth, so you avoid setting them at all.

Guilt operates as the enforcement mechanism. Not natural guilt that arises when you've actually harmed someone, but trained guilt—a conditioned response installed by people who benefited from your limitlessness.

You were taught that having boundaries makes you morally deficient. Selfish. Uncaring. A bad person.

Notice who taught you this. Notice who benefits when you can't say no.

The pattern often manifests as constant accommodation—adjusting your preferences to match whoever you're with, saying yes to invitations you dread, giving time and energy you don't have. It looks like generosity. It functions as self-erasure. You're not actually connecting with people when you do this. You're performing availability to prevent abandonment.

The mechanism underneath is: if I can become whatever they need, they won't have a reason to leave. If I'm useful enough, I'm safe enough.

But this trades one danger for another. You avoid abandonment by abandoning yourself.

Your system has been operating from a specific premise: survival requires having no boundaries. Protection came from being amenable, flexible, small. Any assertion of limits threatened that precarious safety.

The premise isn't true anymore. You're not a child dependent on adults who punish self-advocacy. You're an adult with the option to build relationships with people who respect limits. But your nervous system hasn't updated its threat assessment. It's still running a program designed for an environment you no longer inhabit.

In the beginning, each boundary you set will signal danger to your body. Your stomach will clench. Your thoughts will flood with catastrophic predictions.

This doesn't mean you're doing something wrong. It means you're doing something your system isn't accustomed to—yet.

The response will recalibrate with repetition, with experiences of stating limits and remaining connected, of saying no and not being destroyed.

EXERCISE: Mapping Your Boundary Fear

This exercise uses a spatial approach rather than a list format. You'll create a visual map of what happens in your system when you contemplate setting a boundary.

Part A: The Scenario and Internal Response

Think of a specific situation where you need to set a boundary but haven't. Write it briefly:

____

____

When you imagine setting this boundary, map what happens inside you:

In my body, I feel: (Example: throat closes, stomach drops, hands get cold)

____

____

The catastrophic thought that appears: (Example: They'll never speak to me again, I'll be completely alone)

____

____

Part B: Then vs. Now

What this reminds me of from childhood: (Example: When my mother went silent for days after I said no)

____

____

What was actually dangerous then: ____

____

What's actually at risk now: ____

____

Are they the same? ☐ Yes ☐ No

If different, how: ____

____

____

Identifying Where Your Boundaries Have Been Violated

Most trauma survivors can't immediately point to boundary violations because violations became the baseline. When something happens consistently from childhood onward, your system categorizes it as normal rather than unacceptable. You don't think "my boundaries are being crossed"—you think "this is just how things are."

The recognition often comes through sensation rather than thought. A relationship that leaves you needing two days alone afterward to recover. A weekly phone call that makes your shoulders rise toward your ears. A recurring commitment that triggers a flash of resentment so automatic you barely notice it anymore.

Your body notices what your mind learned to overlook.

Start with irritation. Not the obvious anger that comes from dramatic violations, but the low-grade annoyance you've learned to suppress. The slight tightness in your jaw when someone's telling you what to do. The internal eye-roll when someone asks for something they could handle themselves. The micro-impulse to leave a conversation that you immediately override.

Irritation is data. It signals: something here doesn't align with what I need.

Notice the pattern of depletion. Which relationships leave you drained? Not in the way that deep emotional intimacy can be temporarily tiring, but in a persistent, one-directional way. You finish interactions feeling hollowed rather than nourished. Your energy has been extracted.

Watch for resentment that builds without clear origin. You're angry at someone but can't articulate why because they haven't done anything obviously wrong. The problem isn't a single incident—it's an ongoing pattern where you've been saying yes when you mean no, giving when you're empty, adjusting when you need the other person to adjust.

Physical violations show up in unwanted touch, in people entering your space without permission, in your belongings being used without asking. These are often the easiest to identify because they involve clear physical boundaries.

Emotional violations are harder to spot because they're framed as care. Someone insists on knowing how you're feeling. They press for details you don't want to share. They make you responsible for managing their emotional state—you have to keep them calm, keep them happy, prevent their disappointment. They react to your emotions with criticism or control: you're too angry, too sad, too much.

Time violations appear as chronic disrespect for your schedule. People cancel repeatedly. They're always late. They assume your availability without asking. They expect immediate responses to messages. They treat your time as less valuable than theirs.

Mental violations show up when someone tells you what you think or how you should think. They dismiss your perspective, mock your beliefs, or insist their interpretation of your experience is more accurate than yours. They gaslight—tell you things didn't happen the way you remember, that you're overreacting, that your perception is flawed.

The violation you're most likely to miss is the one involving your energy and capacity. Someone treats you as an infinite resource. They need constant support but never ask if you have capacity to provide it. They dump their problems without checking if you're in a state to receive them. They take your emotional labor for granted.

Watch for the relief you feel when something gets canceled. If your first reaction to a changed plan is not disappointment but a loosening in your chest, a sense of reprieve, that relationship or commitment is violating something.

Notice patterns of dread. You feel heavy before seeing certain people. You find yourself creating excuses to avoid situations. A wave of heat or micro-nausea washes through you when their name appears on your phone. Your body is trying to protect you from something your conscious mind hasn't acknowledged yet.

Sometimes a boundary violation doesn't involve obvious harm. Someone isn't doing anything malicious. But the dynamic still depletes you. They need more than you have to give. The relationship requires constant self-negation to maintain. You can't be yourself around them without tension.

The question isn't whether they're a bad person. The question is whether the dynamic respects your limits.

Ask yourself: Would I want someone I care about to be treated this way? If the answer is no, you've identified a violation—even if you've tolerated it for years.

✏ EXERCISE: Sensation-Based Boundary Recognition

Instead of categorizing violations by type, this exercise uses your body's signals to identify where boundaries need reinforcement.

Step 1: The Body Scan for Relationships

Go through your regular commitments and relationships. For each one, notice what happens in your body when you think about it.

Person/Situation: ____

Body sensation when I think about this: ____

(Examples: shoulders tighten, stomach clenches, feel lighter/heavier, breath changes, sudden warmth, pulsing at temples)

Person/Situation: ____

Body sensation: ____

Person/Situation: ____

Body sensation: ____

Step 2: The Relief Test

Which commitments would make you feel relieved if they were canceled?

____

____

Step 3: The Irritation Pattern

When do you feel that micro-flash of irritation or resentment, even if you immediately suppress it?

____

____

Step 4: Identifying the Specific Crossing

Choose one person or situation from above. What specifically is happening that your body is reacting to?

____

____

____

What would need to change for that sensation to ease?

____

____

____

Setting Limits Without Guilt or Explanation

Setting a boundary isn't a negotiation. You're not requesting permission or opening a discussion about whether your limit is reasonable. You're stating what you will and won't do, what's acceptable and what isn't. The other person's agreement is irrelevant to whether the boundary exists.

This distinction matters because most trauma survivors approach boundaries as if they need justification. You believe you have to explain, convince, prove your boundary is legitimate. You don't.

The internal work happens before you speak. Before you can state a limit clearly, you need to locate it in your body. Where do you feel the "no"? Most people feel it as resistance—a pulling back, a tightening, a sense of wrongness when they imagine saying yes. Find that sensation. Let it be present. Speak from that place rather than from the part of you that wants to smooth things over.

Notice what happens when you imagine stating your boundary plainly, without softening. Your system will likely flood with guilt, with the urge to apologize, with fear that you're being harsh. This is the conditioning—the trained response meant to keep you compliant. You can feel it and still proceed.

A clear boundary has minimal words. The more you explain, the more opportunities you create for debate. "I'm not available for that" is complete. "I can't take that on" is sufficient. You don't need to justify why.

When pressed for explanation: "It doesn't work for me" or "That's not something I'm doing" or simply "I've made other plans." The plans can be rest. They can be nothing. Your time is yours to allocate.

The instinct to apologize comes from the belief that your boundaries inconvenience others, that having limits makes you difficult. Stop beginning with "I'm sorry." You're not sorry for protecting yourself. If you wouldn't apologize for locking your door at night, don't apologize for this.

The instinct to negotiate comes from fear that if you're too firm, the relationship will break. But notice: if a relationship collapses under the weight of a reasonable boundary, it reveals the structure it always had.

When someone pushes back—and they will if they're accustomed to your limitlessness—your work is to stay with your own limit. They might guilt-trip: "I can't believe you're saying no. I thought I could count on you." You repeat the boundary: "I understand you're disappointed. I'm still not available."

They might escalate emotionally: "You're being selfish. You never help anymore." You remain factual: "I hear that you're upset. My answer hasn't changed."

They might negotiate: "What if I just need you for an hour? What if we did it next week instead?" You close the negotiation: "I'm not available for this. That's final."

They might withdraw affection, hoping that emotional punishment will make you reverse the boundary. Let them withdraw. If someone punishes you for having limits, they've shown you who they are.

Some people will use your history against you: "You're just being difficult because of your trauma" or "You're overreacting again." This is manipulation designed to make you question your own perception. Your boundary stands regardless of their interpretation of why you have it.

The technique when someone keeps pushing: say the exact same words in the exact same tone. Don't elaborate, don't defend, don't adjust your phrasing. Become a wall that only says one thing. Eventually they'll either accept it or leave. Both outcomes are fine.

A boundary only exists if your behavior changes when it's crossed. If you state a limit and someone crosses it, there must be a response or the limit means nothing. The response doesn't have to be dramatic. It's often just a natural consequence.

Someone repeatedly shows up late? Stop waiting for them. Someone ignores your request not to discuss certain topics? End the conversation when they bring it up. Someone keeps asking for things after you've said no? Stop responding to those requests.

You don't announce the consequence in advance like a threat. You just implement it. If patterns continue after you've been clear, you reduce contact, share less, or end the relationship. Not as punishment, but as practical adjustment to reality.

Some people will leave when you start setting boundaries. This is information, not failure. They didn't want a relationship with you—they wanted an arrangement where you provide and they receive. That's not a relationship worth maintaining.

The people who stay and adjust are showing you they value you beyond your utility.

EXERCISE: Boundary Rehearsal Through Rewriting

This exercise uses a real past situation to practice boundary language.

Step 1: Choose a Real Incident

Think of a recent time when you didn't set a boundary but wish you had. Describe what happened:

____

____

____

Step 2: Write What You Actually Said

What did you say in the moment?

____

____

Step 3: Notice Your Internal State

What were you feeling in your body when you said yes/accommodated/didn't speak up?

____

____

Step 4: Write the Boundary Version

Now write what you would say if you were to set a clear boundary. Use 15 words or fewer. No apology. No explanation.

____

____

Step 5: Anticipate and Respond

How might they have responded if you'd said that?

____

Your one-sentence reply that repeats the boundary:

____

Step 6: Body-Based Rehearsal

Stand up. Say your boundary statement out loud. Notice what happens in your body. If you feel guilt or fear, let it be present while you say the words anyway. Repeat three times.

Physical sensation after saying it: ____

Protecting Your Energy From People Who Take Too Much

Certain dynamics drain you in a way that's distinct from ordinary tiredness. You spend an hour with someone and need three hours alone afterward just to feel like yourself again. You answer one text message and end up in an exhausting exchange that pulls you away from everything else. You thought you were helping someone but realize you've been taking on their problems as if they're your own.

This isn't about character judgment. It's about recognizing patterns that exceed your capacity.

Some people genuinely don't realize they're taking more than you can give. They're overwhelmed by their own lives and reach for support wherever they can find it. Your willingness to provide becomes the path of least resistance. They're not trying to harm you—they're trying to survive. But their coping strategy is eroding your capacity.

Other people have learned that you won't say no. They've mapped your boundaries and found none. They take because taking is available. These dynamics require different responses, but both require that you stop operating as if your capacity is infinite.

Watch for patterns rather than isolated incidents.

The dynamic where every interaction involves crisis. Something is always urgent, always falling apart, always requiring immediate attention. You become their emergency response system. But emergencies that happen daily aren't emergencies—they're patterns. And the pattern often includes not taking action on the advice you give, which means the crisis recurs and your support gets extracted again.

If someone needs crisis-level support more than occasionally, they need professional help, not your constant availability.

The dynamic where you listen for extended periods but when you need to be heard, the conversation redirects. You've spent months being their sounding board, but when you're struggling, they minimize it, change the subject, or turn it back to their own issues. This stops functioning as a mutual connection—it becomes unpaid emotional labor.

The dynamic where someone asks before sharing but then proceeds regardless of your answer. "Do you have capacity to talk about something hard?" You say no, or you say you only have ten minutes, but then they unload anyway and you end up trapped in a two-hour conversation you didn't consent to. They've learned to ask performatively while ignoring your actual answer.

The dynamic where someone refuses to respect topic boundaries. You've said you're not available to discuss certain things—your relationship, your family, your work decisions—but they keep bringing them up. Each time you have to reinforce the boundary, which takes energy, which is exactly what you were trying to protect.

The dynamic where someone's presence itself is exhausting. They're not asking for anything specific, but being around them depletes you. They're consistently negative, or their energy is chaotic, or they create drama, or they process everything out loud at length. The relationship feels like work even when nothing particular is happening.

These patterns tell you where your boundaries need reinforcement.

You don't have to cut people off entirely unless the relationship is actively harmful. But you can limit exposure. Shorter visits. Less frequent contact. Specific contexts only—seeing them in groups rather than one-on-one, where you're not the sole container for their intensity.

Before engaging, decide your limit. "I have twenty minutes." When twenty minutes is up, you leave—even if they're mid-sentence, even if they seem upset that you're going. Your boundary isn't contingent on their convenience.

You can care about someone's situation without making it your situation. Their crisis is not your crisis. Their emotions are not your emotions. Their problems are not your problems. You can hold space for them briefly, express care, and still decline to carry what's theirs to carry.

Practice: "That sounds really hard. I hope you find what you need." Then exit the conversation.

Some relationships won't survive your boundaries. If the only way someone will stay connected to you is if you have no limits, they're not connected to you—they're connected to what you provide. Losing that relationship reveals what it actually was.

Consider ending relationships where boundaries are consistently violated despite clear communication. Where you feel worse after every interaction. Where your body consistently braces before and collapses after every interaction. Where maintaining the relationship requires you to be less than you are. Where the cost to your wellbeing outweighs any benefit.

You can care about someone and still recognize they're not sustainable for you.

The hardest boundary work is often with yourself. You're the one overcommitting. You're the one scrolling through traumatic content at midnight. You're the one not stopping when your body signals exhaustion. You're the one maintaining relationships that drain you because you feel obligated.

Decide how many commitments you'll hold simultaneously. Block out non-negotiable rest time. Limit how much news or social media you'll consume. End your own patterns of pushing past depletion.

Your system has limits. Ignoring them has a cost.

✎ EXERCISE: Weekly Saturation Check

This exercise creates a regular practice rather than a one-time inventory.

Instructions:

Choose one day each week (Sunday evening works well) to assess your saturation level. Set a recurring reminder.

This Week's Check (Date: __________)

Overall Saturation Level:

Rate your current energy/capacity on a scale where:

1 = Completely run thin, running on empty

5 = Balanced, sustainable

10 = Energized, plenty of capacity

Current level: _____

This Week's Main Drains:

What three things took the most from you this week?

1. ____

2. ____

3. ____

Next Week's Protection:

Based on this week's drains, what one boundary will you implement next week?

The Commitment:

I will protect my capacity next week by:

After Four Weeks:

Look back at your weekly checks. What patterns do you notice? Which drains are recurring? Where do you need structural change rather than weekly adjustments?

This practice makes boundary-setting responsive rather than reactive. You're checking your capacity regularly and adjusting before you reach complete depletion.

Chapter 12: Reclaiming Your Life From Survival Mode

"Healing is not about moving on or getting over it, it's about learning to make peace with our lives and all that has happened." — *Megan Devine*

It's like waking up from a long emergency shift and realizing you don't know how to act when nothing's on fire. The crisis ended, maybe years ago, but you're still running on crisis protocols. You move through spaces calculating threat levels. You keep yourself contained, protected, always ready. Not because danger is present, but because danger was your normal for so long that peace feels foreign.

The strangest part of leaving survival mode isn't the leaving itself. It's discovering you don't know who you are without it. Survival mode gave you a role: protector, fighter, invisible one, fixer. It gave you a purpose: get through today. When that falls away, what's left? Who are you when you're not just trying to make it through?

This disorientation is rarely discussed. You've worked on calming your nervous system, managing flashbacks, building boundaries. Those symptoms might be easing. But there's another transition that happens when they do: the unsettling discovery that you've been so focused on surviving, you never learned to live. You don't have a template for a life that isn't organized around threat.

Living means something different than not-surviving. Not-surviving is the absence of crisis. Living is the presence of something else: engagement, choice, desire, connection that isn't transactional, rest that isn't collapse. Many trauma survivors reach a point where the immediate symptoms have lessened, but they still feel hollow. Safe, maybe, but empty. Stable, but not quite alive.

This chapter is about that specific transition: the space between "I've survived" and "I'm living." It's about the identity confusion that comes when your survival strategies no longer fit your life. It's about learning to recognize safety when it arrives, not just danger when it threatens. It's about building a life designed for growth, not just protection. It's about discovering who you are when you're not in crisis mode.

This isn't about fixing what's broken or returning to some earlier version of yourself that no longer exists in the same form. This is about meeting who you're becoming: someone shaped by trauma but not controlled by it, someone who knows how to survive and is learning how to thrive.

You've done the hardest work already: you survived. Now comes the different work of figuring out what you actually want your life to be.

Moving From Surviving to Actually Living

The transition out of survival mode doesn't feel like relief at first. It feels like vertigo.

You've spent years, maybe decades, operating from a clear mandate: stay safe, avoid danger, protect yourself. Your nervous system had a job, and it did that job relentlessly. Then something shifts. Therapy helps. Time passes. The worst symptoms ease. You're calmer, more regulated, less reactive. You should feel better. Instead, you feel lost.

When crisis was your organizing principle, every decision was clear: Does this keep me safe or put me at risk? Does this person threaten me or not? Can I handle this or will it overwhelm me? Your life had structure, even if that structure was built entirely around threat avoidance.

Without crisis as your compass, everything becomes murky. You can go places without mapping escape routes. You can be with people without monitoring their mood. You can make plans without extensive contingency scenarios. But now what? What do you actually want to do? Who do you want to become? What does a day look like when you're not just trying to get through it?

This is the identity crisis of healing: you've been a survivor for so long, you don't know how to be anything else.

Some people feel this as emptiness, a strange hollowness where all that vigilance used to be. Others feel it as anxiety, the unsettling sense that if you're not watching for danger, something terrible will slip past your defenses. Some feel it as boredom: life without adrenaline feels flat, colorless, too quiet. Some feel it as guilt, like you don't deserve to relax when others are still suffering, or when parts of you are still hurting.

The first sign you're transitioning out of survival mode isn't peace. It's disorientation.

You might notice you panic when everything is calm. Your nervous system, trained to expect threat, interprets quiet as the moment before ambush. You create problems to solve because having nothing to fix feels more dangerous than having a crisis. You pick fights, manufacture drama, or spiral into anxiety about invented scenarios: anything to fill the void where hypervigilance used to live.

You might notice you don't know what you like anymore. Someone asks what you want for dinner, what movie you'd enjoy, how you'd like to spend your weekend, and you draw a blank. You've spent so long accommodating others' needs, avoiding conflict, or just surviving, that you lost track of your own preferences. You don't know what brings you pleasure because pleasure wasn't relevant when you were just trying to stay afloat.

You might notice a strange disconnection from the stability you've built. You have a home, maybe relationships, some safety, but it doesn't feel like it belongs to you. Without the constant threat to define yourself against, you're not sure who inhabits this calmer life. The question "who am I when I'm not surviving?" has no ready answer, and that absence feels more destabilizing than the chaos you knew how to navigate.

You might notice you create false urgency. You overfill your schedule, take on too many projects, manufacture deadlines. Not because these things matter, but because moving fast keeps you from feeling the discomfort of slowing down. Stillness means you might have to face what you've been running from: grief, emptiness, the question of who you are now.

You might notice relationships feel strange without transactions. People offer support without wanting anything back, and you don't know how to receive it. Someone loves you without you having to earn it, and you keep testing them to find the conditions you're sure must exist. Connection that isn't based on utility or survival feels too vulnerable, too exposing.

These aren't signs something's wrong with your healing. These are signs you're in a genuine transition, leaving one way of being without yet knowing the next.

The shift from surviving to living happens through small investigations into what you want.

Survival mode operates on fear: avoid this, protect against that, prevent the other thing. Living mode operates on desire: I want this, I'm curious about that, I'd like to try the other thing. The problem is, you might have no idea what you desire. Decades of suppressing wants for the sake of safety means you've lost the signal.

Start with tiny investigations. Not "What do I want from my life?" but "What do I want for the next five minutes?" Do you want silence or sound? Do you want to move or be still? Do you want to be alone or reach out to someone? These aren't profound questions, but they're practice in tuning into desire rather than just avoiding discomfort.

Track moments when something feels good, not good in the sense of relief that something bad didn't happen, but good in the sense of actual pleasure or interest. Maybe you noticed sunlight on your skin. Maybe a song caught your attention. Maybe you felt genuinely curious about something. These are breadcrumbs leading you toward what you want, not just what you're afraid of.

Practice tolerating the vulnerability of wanting. Every desire creates possibility for disappointment. Every preference creates possibility for not getting what you want. Every choice creates possibility for regret. Survival mode eliminates these risks by eliminating want. Living mode accepts them as the cost of having a life that's yours. Identify one "non-survival" choice you can make this week. Not a choice about safety or protection: a choice about preference. Maybe you try a new food just because you're curious. Maybe you take a walk not for regulation but for enjoyment. Maybe you listen to music not to calm down but because you like it. These choices build the muscle of living rather than just surviving.

Expect discomfort. Your nervous system will protest that paying attention to desire is dangerous, frivolous, selfish. It will tell you that wanting things leads to disappointment, that preferences make you vulnerable, that you should just be grateful for safety. This is your survival programming speaking. Acknowledge it's trying to protect you, then choose the living-mode action anyway.

Notice the difference between safety-seeking and life-building. Safety-seeking asks: How do I avoid pain? Life-building asks: What do I want to create? Both are valid, but if every choice is about avoiding pain, you're still in survival mode. Life-building means occasionally choosing something because you want it, even if it comes with risk. The transition isn't about suddenly knowing who you are or what you want. It's about creating space for those questions to have answers. It's about building a life slowly, through small choices that honor what you're drawn toward, not just what you're running from. You're not trying to become someone new. You're trying to meet who you've always been underneath the survival strategies: the person whose desires, curiosities, and preferences got buried under the need to just make it through.

EXERCISE: Discovering Desire Beyond Survival

Part 1: Survival vs. Living Choices

Look at your last week. List 3 choices you made primarily for safety or to avoid discomfort:

1. ____________________
2. ____________________
3. ____________________

Now list 3 choices you made based on actual preference or desire (if none, write "none yet"):

1. ____________________
2. ____________________
3. ____________________

Part 2: Weekly Desire Map

Once a day for the next week, pause for a moment and notice what you want *right now*—not what feels safest, not what you "should" want, but the first genuine pull you can detect. Each day, complete the sentence below and add a quick check-in to discern whether the "want" is desire or protection.

Day 1:

Right now, I want ____________________

Check: Does this feel like desire or protection? ____________________

Day 2:

Right now, I want ____________________

Check: Does this feel like desire or protection? ____________________

Day 3:

Right now, I want ____

Check: Does this feel like desire or protection? ______________________________

Day 4:

Right now, I want ____

Check: Does this feel like desire or protection? ______________________________

Day 5:

Right now, I want ____

Check: Does this feel like desire or protection? ______________________________

Day 6:

Right now, I want ____

Check: Does this feel like desire or protection? ______________________________

Day 7:

Right now, I want ____

Check: Does this feel like desire or protection? ______________________________

Part 3: One Non-Survival Experiment

Choose one action this week based purely on curiosity, pleasure, or preference (not safety):

I will: ____

Expected discomfort: "My nervous system will tell me __________________________

____"

Part 4: Tracking Life-Building Signals

What happened when you let yourself want something?

____

____

Did anything feel different in your body when you chose preference over protection?

____

____

____

Designing a Life That Honors Your Nervous System

Building a life after trauma isn't about returning to "normal." It's about designing sustainability. Not a life that looks like everyone else's, but a life that works with your nervous system's reality while still allowing growth.

The tension is real: you want to expand what's possible AND you have a nervous system shaped by chronic threat. Pushing too hard retraumatizes. Protecting too much keeps you small. The goal is finding your specific rhythm: the pace at which you can stretch without snapping.

Most advice about "self-care" or "work-life balance" assumes a baseline nervous system capacity that trauma survivors often don't have. You might need more recovery time than others. More solitude. More predictability. More control over your environment. This isn't weakness or dysfunction; it's information about your system's current capacity.

The question isn't "Why do I need so much?" It's "How do I build a life that works with what I actually need right now, while staying open to what becomes possible as I heal?"

Think of your life structure as a framework for expansion, not a cage for protection. A framework provides support that lets you build upward. A cage keeps you contained. The difference is intention and flexibility.

Start by identifying what genuinely supports your regulation versus what's avoidance disguised as self-care. Does staying home alone actually help you regulate, or does it prevent you from practicing connection? Does maintaining rigid routines create safety, or does it keep you from learning you can handle small disruptions? Does limiting social contact protect your energy, or does it reinforce the belief that people are dangerous?

These are hard questions with no universal answers. The same behavior might be regulation for one person and avoidance for another. The test is: Does this choice expand my capacity over time, or keep it the same?

Build in what trauma therapists call "titrated exposure": small, manageable doses of things that stretch your window of tolerance. Maybe you can't handle a full social event, but you can handle coffee with one person for an hour. Maybe you can't tolerate complete spontaneity, but you can handle one unplanned evening per week. Maybe you can't manage open-ended commitments, but you can manage commitments with clear end times.

The goal is finding the edge of your window: the place where you're challenged but not overwhelmed. Too far inside your window and you never grow. Too far outside and you collapse. The edge is where neuroplasticity happens, where your nervous system learns new patterns.

Pay attention to your recovery time. This is the hidden variable most people ignore. You might be able to handle a challenging situation (a difficult conversation, a crowded space, an emotional topic) but how long does it take you to return to baseline afterward? Some trauma survivors need hours of alone time after thirty minutes of socializing. Some need a full day of rest after any emotionally intense experience. Some need physical movement to process, while others need complete stillness.

Track your actual recovery time, not what you think it should be. Then design your life around that reality. If you know a dinner with family requires six hours of recovery, don't schedule work commitments the next morning. If you know therapy sessions leave you raw for a day, protect that day. This is the rhythm that keeps your internal structure from collapsing.

Create what trauma therapists call "dual awareness": the ability to be in an experience while staying connected to your grounded self. This is how you expand capacity without getting overwhelmed. You attend the event, but you also keep one foot in your body, checking in with your nervous system. You have the difficult conversation, but you also maintain awareness of your window's edge. You try something new, but you also know your exit strategy.

Dual awareness lets you stay in growth experiences longer because you're monitoring your system in real time. When you notice yourself approaching the edge of your window, you can use regulation tools before you tip into overwhelm. This is how your window gradually expands: through repeated experiences of "I stretched, I noticed my limit, I regulated, and I was okay."

Design your environment as a regulation tool. Your physical space isn't neutral; it either supports or undermines your nervous system. You might need a space that's entirely yours, where you control lighting, sound, temperature, visual input. You might need specific textures available: soft blankets, comfortable seating. You might need to minimize visual clutter because your nervous system processes every object as potential information to track. The less energy your system spends on environmental processing, the more capacity you have freed up for actual living.

Build rituals that mark transitions. Trauma survivors often struggle with shifting between states: from work to home, from social to solitary, from activated to calm. Your nervous system needs help recognizing that one context is ending and another beginning. Create small rituals: a specific route you walk, a piece of clothing you change, a song you play, five minutes of a specific grounding practice. These cues help your system shift gears instead of staying stuck in one mode.

The most important design principle: build in permission to recalibrate. No life structure works perfectly all the time. You'll have periods where you need more support, more solitude, more structure. You'll have periods where you can handle more stimulation, more spontaneity, more challenge. Rigidity keeps you stuck. Flexibility lets you grow.

Check in quarterly: Is my current life structure still serving me, or have my needs changed? Am I protecting myself appropriately, or am I playing it too safe? Am I stretching toward growth, or am I pushing too hard? Adjust accordingly.

You're not building a life that eliminates all discomfort. You're building a life that creates enough stability that you can tolerate the discomfort of growth. That's the foundation from which healing expands: not perfect safety, but sustainable challenge.

EXERCISE: Your Life Sustainability Map

Part 1: Four Domains Assessment

Place aspects of your current life in these categories:

Resource-Depleting (exhausts without growth)

____

____

____

Resource-Building (genuinely supportive)

____

____

____

Capacity-Expanding (challenging but good)

____

____

____

Capacity-Stagnating (too comfortable/safe)

____

____

____

Part 2: Recovery Time Reality Check

After these experiences, how long do I actually need to return to baseline?

Social interaction: ______________________________

Difficult conversation: ______________________________

Therapy or processing work: ______________________________

Work stress: ______________________________

Unexpected changes: ______________________________

Part 3: Edge of Window Practice

Describe one situation that puts you at the edge of your window (challenging but manageable):

How do you know you're at the edge vs. outside your window?

Part 4: One Structural Adjustment

Based on this map, what's one change that would make your life more sustainable for growth?

Building Resilience Through Post-Traumatic Growth

Something happens in the stillness after survival. When your nervous system finally stops running, when the immediate crisis has passed, when you've done enough healing work to catch your breath, there's a moment of discovering what emerged while you were just trying to survive.

You notice you can sit with silence now. Not the frozen silence of dissociation, but actual quietude. You notice you can think about the future without only imagining disasters. You notice you can stay with contradictions without collapsing: that two opposing things can both be true. You notice you've developed capacities you didn't have before trauma, not because trauma was good, but because you metabolized something devastating into something you can use.

This is post-traumatic growth, but not the sanitized version that shows up in inspirational quotes. This is the gritty version: where strength and fragility coexist, where you're proud of your resilience and grieving what it cost you, where you've gained capacities you wish you didn't need.

The growth that matters most isn't about becoming stronger or more successful. It's about the emergence of capacities that only become possible when you stop fighting for your life.

You can slow down now. This sounds simple, but it's profound. When you're in survival mode, everything is urgent. Every decision is life-or-death. Every interaction is high-stakes. You operate at crisis speed constantly. When that finally ends, you discover you can move at a different pace. You can deliberate. You can reflect. You can let decisions take time. This isn't laziness or avoidance; it's reclaiming your relationship with time.

You can tolerate not knowing. Trauma demands certainty because uncertainty means danger. You had to know where threats were coming from, what people meant, what would happen next. Living in constant ambiguity was impossible. Now, gradually, you find you can hold questions without immediately needing answers. You can sit with "I don't know yet" without panic. You can let things unfold. This is huge: the ability to be present with uncertainty without your nervous system screaming that you must solve it immediately.

You can appreciate ordinary moments. When life is crisis, you don't notice small beauty. You can't afford to. Your attention is survival-focused. When crisis lifts, suddenly you see things: light on water, a particular quality of air, the way someone laughs, food that tastes good, physical comfort. Not because these things are new, but because you finally have the bandwidth to notice them. This isn't toxic positivity. It's reclaimed presence.

You can hold space for others differently. Your understanding of suffering isn't theoretical anymore. You know what it feels like to be trapped, terrified, alone. This creates a specific kind of compassion, not pity or fixing, but genuine witnessing. You can sit with other people's pain without needing to make it better or make it about you. You can offer the kind of presence you needed when you were in the worst of it.

You can feel the openness of multiple possible directions. When you're in survival mode, you can only imagine two futures: the one where you survive and the one where you don't. Everything collapses into binary. When that loosens, you discover you can sense complexity: multiple possible paths, different versions of who you might become, various ways life could unfold. This expansion of possibility is its own form of growth.

You can choose what you're oriented toward. In survival mode, you're oriented toward threat detection. Your attention goes automatically to what could hurt you, who's dangerous, where the exits are. You had to. As you heal, you discover you can redirect attention. You can notice what's working, who's trustworthy, where safety exists. This isn't denial of danger; it's recalibration toward a fuller reality that includes both threat and goodness.

This growth doesn't happen because you worked for it or because you're special. It happens because human nervous systems are designed to adapt. You spent years adapting to constant threat. Now your system is adapting to increasing safety. The adaptations that emerge in safety look like: capacity for stillness, tolerance for uncertainty, attention to beauty, presence with pain, imagination of possibility, and choice about focus.

You don't owe anyone growth. You don't have to find silver linings or make trauma "worth it." The trauma was not worth it. What happened to you was wrong and shouldn't have happened. AND if growth emerged anyway, you can acknowledge it without justifying what caused it.

Some people don't experience post-traumatic growth, and that's completely valid. Some people heal back to a stable baseline without developing new capacities, and that's enough. Some people remain more symptomatic even with treatment, and they're not failing. Growth is not required. Surviving is sufficient.

But if you do notice capacities emerging that weren't there before, if you find you can do things or feel things or hold things you couldn't in the past, that's real. You can name it without making the trauma that caused it good.

The question becomes: Now that these capacities exist, what do you want to do with them? How do you want to use your ability to slow down, to tolerate uncertainty, to notice beauty, to witness pain, to imagine possibility? These aren't just personal qualities; they're resources you can direct toward building the life you want.

You survived what shouldn't have happened. Now you're discovering who you're becoming in the aftermath. Not who you would have been without trauma (that person is gone, and grieving them is legitimate). But who you actually are now, with all you've been through and all you've learned about yourself. That person exists. They're worth knowing.

EXERCISE: Capacities That Emerged in Safety

Part 1: What Can You Do Now?

Think about capacities you've developed that you didn't have before. These aren't talents or skills; they're ways of being:

One thing I can tolerate now that I couldn't before:

____

One way I can be present now that I couldn't before:

____

One thing I can notice now that I couldn't before:

____

Part 2: A Concrete Scene

Describe one specific recent moment where you responded differently than you would have a year ago. Use sensory detail: what did you see, hear, feel in your body?

____

____

What does this scene show you about yourself?

____

____

Part 3: Directing Your Capacities

Choose one capacity you've developed. How do you want to use it going forward?

Capacity: ____

I want to use this to: ____

____

____

____

Your Personal Roadmap for Continued Healing

Healing doesn't end; it becomes integrated into how you live. The work shifts from "fixing what's broken" to "building what I want." From "reducing symptoms" to "expanding capacity." From "getting through the day" to "creating a life I want to inhabit."

You're past the crisis stage. You have tools. You understand your nervous system. You've processed some of the trauma, regulated some of the symptoms, built some capacity. Now what?

Now you design for emergence: creating conditions where the person you're becoming can develop without you having to know in advance who that is.

Think of healing like tending fermentation. You've done the initial work of preparing the conditions, mixing the ingredients, setting things in motion. But the transformation happens in its own time. Check too frequently and you disrupt the process. Ignore it and it spoils. The work now is maintaining conditions that allow change to complete: paying attention without forcing, adjusting as needed, trusting the process has its own intelligence.

Start by identifying what's emerging. Not what you want to become, but what's already beginning to show up. Maybe you're noticing moments of curiosity about things that used to feel dangerous. Maybe you're experimenting with connection that isn't based on utility. Maybe you're making choices based on preference rather than just protection. These aren't goals; they're shoots breaking through soil. Your job is to notice them and create conditions where they can grow.

Ask: What's trying to emerge in me right now? Not "What should I be?" but "What's already surfacing that needs support?"

Build rituals that support emergence. Not routines that maintain stability (though those matter), but practices that create space for what's new. Maybe it's weekly reflection time where you notice changes you wouldn't see day-to-day. Maybe it's monthly experiments with something outside your usual patterns. Maybe it's quarterly reassessment of whether your life structure still fits who you're becoming.

The difference between stability practices and emergence practices:

- Stability practices maintain your baseline (grounding, boundaries, regulation)
- Emergence practices support growth (trying new things, expanding capacity, building identity)

You need both. Stability without emergence keeps you stuck. Emergence without stability leads to collapse.

Identify your co-regulation resources. This is different from general support. Co-regulation means people whose nervous systems help regulate yours: whose calm affects your calm, whose presence helps you access states you can't reach alone. You might have a therapist who does this. You might have a friend whose way of being helps you settle. You might have a partner whose steadiness you can borrow when yours wavers.

Who are your co-regulation resources? Not just "who supports you" but specifically "whose nervous system helps regulate yours?"

Map your identity evolution. Not who you were before trauma (that person is gone) and not who you "should" be (that's probably internalized expectations). Who are you becoming as someone who survived trauma and is choosing what comes next?

This isn't a fixed identity to achieve. It's tracking a direction: What values are becoming important to you? What parts of yourself feel most authentic? What kind of life are you drawn toward? Let this be a living document that changes as you do.

Build flexibility into every plan. The roadmap you create today will need adjustment next month. Your needs will change. New capacities will emerge. Old symptoms might resurface. Things you thought were solid might shift. This isn't failure; it's how healing actually works. Linear paths are fantasy. Actual healing moves like weather patterns: influenced by multiple systems, sometimes predictable, often surprising.

Instead of rigid goals, set directional intentions. Not "I will have zero flashbacks" but "I'm moving toward less reactivity." Not "I will trust people completely" but "I'm practicing vulnerability in small doses." Not "I will be healed" but "I'm building capacity gradually."

Create your emergency grounding protocol. Not if setbacks happen: when. Triggers are guaranteed. Having a pre-planned response means you don't have to figure it out while dysregulated.

My Emergency Grounding Protocol:

First anchor: ______________________________

Second anchor: ______________________________

Third anchor: ______________________________

What I need to remember during hard times: ______________________________

____

Track subtle progress. You won't feel dramatically different day-to-day. The changes that matter are often invisible until you look back across months. Create markers for noticing: How you handled a trigger this month compared to six months ago. How long recovery takes now versus before. How much presence you can maintain. How often you access genuine pleasure. How relationships feel different. These micro-shifts accumulate into transformation.

Design for your future self. The person you're becoming will have different needs than you have right now. Build in adaptation: Check in regularly. Adjust your structure as capacity changes. Release practices that no longer serve. Add new ones as they become relevant. Stay in conversation with who you're becoming, not attached to who you were.

You're not aiming for perfect. You're not trying to eliminate all trauma responses or reach some healed endpoint. You're building a life where trauma is integrated: present but not dominant, informing but not controlling, part of your story but not the whole thing.

The work continues. It becomes less about fixing and more about building. Less about symptoms and more about life. Less about what happened to you and more about who you're choosing to be now.

You've survived. You've begun healing. Now you're stepping into whatever comes next, not because you're done, but because you're ready to meet your life as it actually is, with all its complexity, difficulty, and possibility.

EXERCISE: Designing for Emergence

Part 1: What's Emerging

What's beginning to surface in you that wasn't there before? (Not goals: actual observations)

____

____

____

Part 2: Life Flow Map

Track these elements of your current experience:

What I'm Releasing

(patterns that no longer serve)

____

____

What I'm Building

(new capacities, practices, ways of being)

____

____

What I'm Learning

(insights about myself, my needs, what's possible)

____

____

Who Helps Me Regulate

(co-regulation resources)

____

____

Part 3: Directional Intentions

Choose 2-3 directions (not fixed goals) for the next six months:

1. I'm moving toward: ____
2. I'm practicing: ____
3. I'm building capacity for: ____

Part 4: Adaptation Check-In

Set three dates to reassess this roadmap:

One month: ____

Three months: ____

Six months: ____

At each check-in ask: What's changed? What needs adjusting? What's emerging now?

Part 5: Message to the Version of You Who Will Hold What Emerges Next

Write a brief message to the version of yourself who will read this six months from now. What do you want to remember? What are you hoping will be different? What do you need to hear if things are hard?

Before You Close This Page

"One of the greatest diseases is to be nobody to anybody." – Mother Teresa

The work you've done in this workbook isn't insignificant. You've faced your patterns, tried uncomfortable exercises, and spent time understanding responses that most people will never have to think about. That takes real effort.

Here's something that takes considerably less effort but could help someone who's currently struggling: leaving an honest review on Amazon.

When you describe your experience with this workbook, you're giving future readers the context they need. They want to know if this book addresses their specific symptoms. They want to hear from someone who actually used the exercises, not just read the description.

Your review helps:

- One more person find tools for managing emotional flashbacks
- One more nervous system learn it can settle
- One more trauma survivor realize healing is possible

Would you take three minutes to share your honest thoughts? I read every review personally and genuinely value all feedback, whether positive or critical.

Thank you for your time and for trusting this workbook with your healing process.

Bibliography

Ainsworth, M. D. S., Blehar, M. C., Waters, E., & Wall, S. (1978). *Patterns of Attachment: A Psychological Study of the Strange Situation*. Lawrence Erlbaum.

Becker-Phelps, L. (2014). *Insecure in Love: How Anxious Attachment Can Make You Feel Jealous, Needy, and Worried and What You Can Do About It*. New Harbinger Publications.

Bowlby, J. (1969). *Attachment and Loss, Vol. 1: Attachment*. Basic Books.

Bowlby, J. (1988). *A Secure Base: Parent-Child Attachment and Healthy Human Development*. Basic Books.

Brach, T. (2003). *Radical Acceptance: Embracing Your Life With the Heart of a Buddha*. Bantam.

Brach, T. (2013). *True Refuge: Finding Peace and Freedom in Your Own Awakened Heart*. Bantam.

Brown, B. (2010). *The Gifts of Imperfection: Let Go of Who You Think You're Supposed to Be and Embrace Who You Are*. Hazelden Publishing.

Brown, B. (2012). *Daring Greatly: How the Courage to Be Vulnerable Transforms the Way We Live, Love, Parent, and Lead*. Avery.

Brown, B. (2015). *Rising Strong: How the Ability to Reset Transforms the Way We Live, Love, Parent, and Lead*. Random House.

Brown, B. (2017). *Braving the Wilderness: The Quest for True Belonging and the Courage to Stand Alone*. Random House.

Cameron, J. (1992). *The Artist's Way: A Spiritual Path to Higher Creativity*. TarcherPerigee.

Chodron, P. (1997). *When Things Fall Apart: Heart Advice for Difficult Times*. Shambhala.

Chodron, P. (2001). *The Places That Scare You: A Guide to Fearlessness in Difficult Times*. Shambhala.

Cori, J. L. (2007). *The Emotionally Absent Mother: A Guide to Self-Healing and Getting the Love You Missed*. The Experiment.

Cozolino, L. (2010). *The Neuroscience of Psychotherapy: Healing the Social Brain* (2nd ed.). W. W. Norton & Company.

Dana, D. (2018). *The Polyvagal Theory in Therapy: Engaging the Rhythm of Regulation*. W. W. Norton & Company.

Dana, D. (2020). *Polyvagal Exercises for Safety and Connection: 50 Client-Centered Practices*. W. W. Norton & Company.

Devine, M. (2017). *It's OK That You're Not OK: Meeting Grief and Loss in a Culture That Doesn't Understand*. Sounds True.

Earley, J. (2009). *Self-Therapy: A Step-By-Step Guide to Creating Wholeness and Healing Your Inner Child Using IFS*. Pattern System Books.

Earley, J., & Weiss, B. (2013). *Freedom from Your Inner Critic: A Self-Therapy Approach*. Sounds True.

Engel, B. (2002). *The Power of Apology: Healing Steps to Transform All Your Relationships*. Wiley.

Fisher, J. (2017). *Healing the Fragmented Selves of Trauma Survivors: Overcoming Internal Self-Alienation*. Routledge.

Fosha, D. (2000). *The Transforming Power of Affect: A Model for Accelerated Change*. Basic Books.

Germer, C. K. (2009). *The Mindful Path to Self-Compassion: Freeing Yourself from Destructive Thoughts and Emotions*. Guilford Press.

Germer, C. K., & Neff, K. D. (2019). *Teaching the Mindful Self-Compassion Program: A Guide for Professionals*. Guilford Press.

Gilbert, P. (2009). *The Compassionate Mind: A New Approach to Life's Challenges*. New Harbinger Publications.

Graham, M. (1991). *Blood Memory: An Autobiography*. Doubleday.

Hanson, R. (2013). *Hardwiring Happiness: The New Brain Science of Contentment, Calm, and Confidence*. Harmony.

Hanson, R., & Mendius, R. (2009). *Buddha's Brain: The Practical Neuroscience of Happiness, Love, and Wisdom*. New Harbinger Publications.

Heller, L., & LaPierre, A. (2012). *Healing Developmental Trauma: How Early Trauma Affects Self-Regulation, Self-Image, and the Capacity for Relationship*. North Atlantic Books.

Herman, J. L. (1992). *Trauma and Recovery: The Aftermath of Violence—From Domestic Abuse to Political Terror*. Basic Books.

Johnson, S. (2008). *Hold Me Tight: Seven Conversations for a Lifetime of Love*. Little, Brown Spark.

Kabat-Zinn, J. (1990). *Full Catastrophe Living: Using the Wisdom of Your Body and Mind to Face Stress, Pain, and Illness*. Delacorte Press.

Katherine, A. (2000). *Boundaries: Where You End and I Begin*. Hazelden Publishing.

Knipe, J. (2015). *EMDR Toolbox: Theory and Treatment of Complex PTSD and Dissociation*. Springer Publishing Company.

Lamott, A. (1995). *Bird by Bird: Some Instructions on Writing and Life*. Anchor.

Levine, A., & Heller, R. (2010). *Attached: The New Science of Adult Attachment and How It Can Help You Find—and Keep—Love*. TarcherPerigee.

Levine, P. A. (1997). *Waking the Tiger: Healing Trauma*. North Atlantic Books.

Levine, P. A. (2010). *In an Unspoken Voice: How the Body Releases Trauma and Restores Goodness*. North Atlantic Books.

Levine, P. A. (2015). *Trauma and Memory: Brain and Body in a Search for the Living Past*. North Atlantic Books.

Linehan, M. M. (2014). *DBT Skills Training Manual* (2nd ed.). Guilford Press.

Maté, G. (2003). *When the Body Says No: The Cost of Hidden Stress*. Wiley.

Maté, G. (2008). *In the Realm of Hungry Ghosts: Close Encounters with Addiction*. North Atlantic Books.

Maté, G. (2022). *The Myth of Normal: Trauma, Illness, and Healing in a Toxic Culture*. Avery.

Miller, A. (1981). *The Drama of the Gifted Child: The Search for the True Self*. Basic Books.

Nakazawa, D. J. (2015). *Childhood Disrupted: How Your Biography Becomes Your Biology, and How You Can Heal*. Atria Books.

Neff, K. (2011). *Self-Compassion: The Proven Power of Being Kind to Yourself*. William Morrow.

Neff, K., & Germer, C. (2018). *The Mindful Self-Compassion Workbook: A Proven Way to Accept Yourself, Build Inner Strength, and Thrive*. Guilford Press.

Nhat Hanh, T. (1975). *The Miracle of Mindfulness: An Introduction to the Practice of Meditation*. Beacon Press.

Nhat Hanh, T. (1987). *Being Peace*. Parallax Press.

Ogden, P., & Fisher, J. (2015). *Sensorimotor Psychotherapy: Interventions for Trauma and Attachment*. W. W. Norton & Company.

Ogden, P., Minton, K., & Pain, C. (2006). *Trauma and the Body: A Sensorimotor Approach to Psychotherapy*. W. W. Norton & Company.

Payne, P., Levine, P. A., & Crane-Godreau, M. A. (2015). Somatic experiencing: Using interoception and proprioception as core elements of trauma therapy. *Frontiers in Psychology*, 6, 93.

Perel, E. (2017). *The State of Affairs: Rethinking Infidelity*. Harper.

Porges, S. W. (2011). *The Polyvagal Theory: Neurophysiological Foundations of Emotions, Attachment, Communication, and Self-*

Regulation. W. W. Norton & Company.

Porges, S. W. (2017). *The Pocket Guide to the Polyvagal Theory: The Transformative Power of Feeling Safe*. W. W. Norton & Company.

Rosenberg, M. B. (2003). *Nonviolent Communication: A Language of Life* (2nd ed.). PuddleDancer Press.

Rothschild, B. (2000). *The Body Remembers: The Psychophysiology of Trauma and Trauma Treatment*. W. W. Norton & Company.

Salzberg, S. (1995). *Lovingkindness: The Revolutionary Art of Happiness*. Shambhala.

Salzberg, S. (2011). *Real Happiness: The Power of Meditation*. Workman Publishing.

Schwartz, A. (2013). *The Complex PTSD Workbook: A Mind-Body Approach to Regaining Emotional Control and Becoming Whole*. Althea Press.

Schwartz, R. C. (1995). *Internal Family Systems Therapy*. Guilford Press.

Schwartz, R. C., & Sweezy, M. (2019). *Internal Family Systems Therapy* (2nd ed.). Guilford Press.

Shapiro, F. (2001). *Eye Movement Desensitization and Reprocessing (EMDR): Basic Principles, Protocols, and Procedures* (2nd ed.). Guilford Press.

Siegel, D. J. (1999). *The Developing Mind: How Relationships and the Brain Interact to Shape Who We Are*. Guilford Press.

Siegel, D. J. (2007). *The Mindful Brain: Reflection and Attunement in the Cultivation of Well-Being*. W. W. Norton & Company.

Siegel, D. J. (2010). *Mindsight: The New Science of Personal Transformation*. Bantam.

Siegel, D. J. (2012). *The Developing Mind: How Relationships and the Brain Interact to Shape Who We Are* (2nd ed.). Guilford Press.

Siegel, D. J., & Bryson, T. P. (2011). *The Whole-Brain Child: 12 Revolutionary Strategies to Nurture Your Child's Developing Mind*. Bantam.

Siegel, D. J., & Hartzell, M. (2003). *Parenting from the Inside Out: How a Deeper Self-Understanding Can Help You Raise Children Who Thrive*. TarcherPerigee.

Tatkin, S. (2011). *Wired for Love: How Understanding Your Partner's Brain and Attachment Style Can Help You Defuse Conflict and Build a Secure Relationship*. New Harbinger Publications.

Tedeschi, R. G., & Calhoun, L. G. (2004). *Posttraumatic Growth: Conceptual Foundations and Empirical Evidence*. *Psychological Inquiry*, *15*(1), 1-18.

van der Hart, O., Nijenhuis, E. R. S., & Steele, K. (2006). *The Haunted Self: Structural Dissociation and the Treatment of Chronic Traumatization*. W. W. Norton & Company.

van der Kolk, B. (2014). *The Body Keeps the Score: Brain, Mind, and Body in the Healing of Trauma*. Viking.

Walker, P. (2013). *Complex PTSD: From Surviving to Thriving*. CreateSpace.

Whitfield, C. L. (1987). *Healing the Child Within: Discovery and Recovery for Adult Children of Dysfunctional Families*. Health Communications.

Winnicott, D. W. (1965). *The Maturational Processes and the Facilitating Environment: Studies in the Theory of Emotional Development*. International Universities Press.

Yehuda, R., & LeDoux, J. (2007). Response variation following trauma: A translational neuroscience approach to understanding PTSD. *Neuron*, *56*(1), 19-32.

www.ingramcontent.com/pod-product-compliance
Lightning Source LLC
LaVergne TN
LVHW062126200926
848484LV00007B/1776
9781806472338